"Occasionally you pick up a book that you simply can't put down. *I Choose Brave* was one of those books for me. Not only because Katie Westenberg tells such a powerful story, but because her words inspire both beauty and bravery in the same breath. You will not want to miss this life-changing message."

—Lisa Jacobson, author, cohost of Faithful Life podcast,
founder of Club31Women.com

"On a topic that is often confusing and intimidating—the fear of God—Katie speaks biblical truth. *I Choose Brave* combines riveting storytelling with theological depth. Every Christian struggling to understand what the Bible says about fear should read this book."

—Phylicia Masonheimer, author
of *Stop Calling Me Beautiful*

"If you are walking through a hard place in your life, struggling with fear, or feeling overwhelmed by a mountain ahead of you, Katie's book will serve as a welcome reminder to fear God and walk in faith. Her words challenged and convicted me to say yes to boldly believe God, and choose bravery in spite of my own fear."

—Crystal Paine, *New York Times* bestselling author,
podcaster, and founder of MoneySavingMom.com

"In a world filled with empty promises and self-help mantras, Katie's message rings both countercultural and scripturally sound: True courage begins with proper fear. It's only when our hearts begin to grasp the immensity of our Lord God and the beauty of His matchless character that we dare step into the challenges of daily life. Pick up this book and discover your hope, your courage, and your brave in Christ alone."

—Asheritah Ciuciu, author of *Unwrapping the Names of Jesus* and *Bible and Breakfast: 31 Mornings with Jesus*

"Fear. It's a feeling we all know too well, though we'd rather not. In Scripture we read 'fear not' right alongside 'fear God.' How can those two things coexist? That is the question Katie so beautifully answers, and in the answer, we find the key to living fearless and free."

—Jeannie Cunnion, author of *Mom Set Free*

"Fear has a way of knocking us down and telling us who we are. But we don't have to let fear win! *I Choose Brave* is an invitation to face our fears head on and find freedom in an unlikely place—the fear of God. If you are looking for an honest, biblically rich companion to walk alongside you in your journey toward a braver life, this book is for you!"

—Ruth Schwenk, founder of TheBetterMom.com and coauthor of *In a Boat in the Middle of a Lake: Trusting the God Who Meets Us in Our Storm*

I Choose Brave

EMBRACING HOLY COURAGE AND UNDERSTANDING GODLY FEAR

KATIE WESTENBERG

BETHANYHOUSE
a division of Baker Publishing Group
Minneapolis, Minnesota

© 2020 by Katie Westenberg

Published by Bethany House Publishers
11400 Hampshire Avenue South
Bloomington, Minnesota 55438
www.bethanyhouse.com

Bethany House Publishers is a division of
Baker Publishing Group, Grand Rapids, Michigan

Printed in the United States of America

Library of Congress Cataloging-in-Publication Data
Names: Westenberg, Katie, author.
Title: I choose brave : embracing holy courage and understanding Godly fear / Katie
    Westenberg.
Description: Minneapolis, Minnesota : Bethany House Publishers, [2020]
Identifiers: LCCN 2019056903 | ISBN 9780764235412 (trade paperback) |
    ISBN 9781493424931 (ebook)
Subjects: LCSH: Fear of God—Biblical teaching. | Fear of God—Christianity—
    Meditations. | Courage—Religious aspects—Christianity—Meditations.
Classification: LCC BS680.F42 W48 2020 | DDC 241/.4—dc23
LC record available at https://lccn.loc.gov/2019056903

Cover design by Kara Klontz

Published in association with Tawny Johnson of Illuminate Literary Agency, www.illuminateliterary.com.

20 21 22 23 24 25 26   7 6 5 4 3 2

FOR MY DAUGHTER

Alison.

I'm not sure how a girl I held
Only once could arrest my heart for a
Lifetime, but I am changed because of you.
Your life brought me to my knees, to the end
Of me, in a way nothing else has. And in that
End, I came face to face with a Holy
God, true freedom in fearing Him.
I am wholly grateful to Him for you.
May these words pay tribute to your
Brief life and bring glory to the only
One worthy. Until I hold you again, Mom.

Contents

Foreword

Two years ago, on an uncharacteristically chilly June afternoon, I received results that showed a mass on my kidney. According to my doctor, a mass on the kidney is difficult to biopsy. "It's best to wait and watch," she advised.

The prescription: Six months of waiting to see if this mass changed size or shape. If it did, it could indicate cancer. If it didn't, more wait and watch.

At the time, six people called me Mom. We were granting my teenage daughters new independence all while teaching my toddler to write his letters. My littlest daughter spoke a handful of words. Time couldn't stop in our home for things like potential diagnoses. Diapers needed changing. Teenage hormones needed tending and care. Dinner wasn't optional.

But my mind . . . my mind roiled with the what-ifs. I refused to search online, and yet the inklings of information I gathered (before restricting myself) haunted my thinking. I tucked my little girl into bed at night, wondering if I would see her wedding day.

That summer, we frequented the pool at the Y, made memories on the soft sand of Hilton Head Island, and Nate and I hiked the Rockies—all while fear crouched. Fear isn't a gentleman; it doesn't respect boundaries. There is no vacation from fear.

But I discovered—as a latent fear that had haunted many of my days before the now undeniable ultrasound (it now had a name and a face)—that much more potent than the thousands of thoughts racing through my mind each day were God's thoughts about himself.

He had answers for my fear in His Word. He had a new fear for me as I found Him there.

The last morning of our three-day stay in Estes Park, Nate and I hiked up to Bierstadt Lake. I sat at the water's edge, struck by the size of the mountains against my fear. My view gave me proper proportion.

I pleaded with God: *Disentangle me from this fear. Relieve me from this web of fear.* I'd asked Him that same thing for months, over many conversations, and yet that morning of prayer hangs suspended in my memory like a snow globe.

Sometimes we need a mountain in the background to enable us to remember a particular conversation with God.

And He came. I didn't garner new attention from Him with my little mountain view, but over weeks and months (many prayed in adoration as I worked my way through Psalm 18, verse by verse, that summer), He received my cries. At the end of my six months of "wait and watch," I wept over the steering wheel on my drive to the follow-up ultrasound. "You did it, God. You did what I didn't think you could do," I kept saying as I choked back my tears.

He replaced my fear with early seeds of the fear of Him.

The ending of that time was not the results of my ultrasound. Instead, it was the shift in my perspective about God. It was the shift in my heart toward Him. He replaced my fear with himself. I saw His kind eyes during those fearful months. He cupped His hand around my bleeding heart, and I felt it. He whispered into my dark.

He held me in my fear. And this was even before I found out the results.

When the ultrasound tech said to me, bewildered, "Well, ma'am, there is nothing there. Are you certain they detected a mass six months ago?" the story remained: God healed my fear. Bigger than His touch to my body were His hands holding my fearful heart. My *watching and waiting* were more about His near-movement in my heart than about my body.

And so all these months later, I read the words Katie—this friend and storyteller and Truth whisperer—writes, and I wish I'd had this book in my hands the summer of my "wait and watch."

What you are about to read is the story of a woman who discovered the beautiful, wild fear of God in her dark night.

And yet it's your story too. And mine. Reading these pages feels like sitting with a sage over coffee and learning language, from His Word and from this friend, for what our heart most craves.

Settle in. These may be your months of "wait and watch."

Sara Hagerty, bestselling author of
Every Bitter Thing Is Sweet, Unseen, and *Adore*

Introduction
MORE THAN A BETTER PONYTAIL

It's odd to me that we call it the *Holy Bible*, those very words embossed in gold on some variation of a leather cover—our lamp and light as Proverbs says—and yet we let it lie dusty, shelved. A lamp without oil, bereft of power. The light we don't utilize, don't understand, isn't all that helpful, is it? We still walk blind.

Perhaps we could run our fingers along its passages and write our name in the dust of all we skim over, breeze past, because does it really even matter in the here and now? We read over passages like 1 Samuel 12:24: "Only fear the LORD, and serve Him in truth with all your heart; for consider what great things He has done for you." Um, okay. *With all my heart.* Great things, yes. I get it. *Sort of.*

Scriptures like this have given me pause in recent years. *Only fear the Lord?* What exactly does that mean? When I began to see how much that very command is woven into Scripture, I wondered, *Why am I okay with the not knowing? This must matter, right?*

There is the tangible definition of fear you and I both know. You know what it's like, how it feels, when the truly scary diagnosis hits close to home—when it's *your* grandmother, *your* daughter, *your* spouse or parent or friend, or *you.* You know how the whole world feels paper-thin, fragile. You know the vulnerability of bad things happening to good people when it could have just as easily been you. When you don't know if the next paycheck will be enough and the news headlines tell of another school or church that was shot up. You begin to wonder if anything, *anything,* is safe or sacred anymore. It's scary. That fear is a well-worn pair of jeans, sliding on easily, consuming your thoughts slowly, comfortably almost.

But fear the Lord? That doesn't even make sense, does it? Stay tuned; we'll go there.

At the same time, we know the tired replay when that familiar fear feels suffocating. The memes and straight-talk books tell us to dig deep, to look inside, to fix your ponytail and carry on. That's cute on a social media graphic, but friend, have you actually tried fixing your ponytail and carrying on when the fear is malignant? When the doctor tells you, "I'm sorry, but your baby is not going to live"? I have. I could have pulled that ponytail until I had slits for eyes and I'd still be scared. Really stinking scared. With a ponytail headache.

That junction led me here—to a place of desperately wanting to know Him both *in* and *through* my worst fears—of being alone, of losing people I love, of it all not being what I consider okay in the end. It led me to dust off who the Word of God says He is and how we are called to respond.

I'm a girl who believes fervently in the living and active Word of God and wants that inspired Word to become living and active in me. *In you.* But I sometimes wonder how? *How*—if it becomes commonplace to continually skim over and water down. *How*—if we play to cultural trends and seek to make the Word of God more palatable in our time and space.

If this Word truly is a light and a lamp, can we pick it up, take it in, and ask the Holy Spirit to use these words to show us a way to fight fear and find freedom that lasts longer than a tight ponytail? Can we ask Him what real courage is, what real fear is, and expect Him to answer? Can we trust Him to wash away the cultural chaff, the yeast, and show us what is true? Can we believe Him for answers that are every bit as applicable in the here and now, our real and present struggles, as they were in the biblical stories most of us have known since childhood?

Without a doubt, the answer is yes. Our immutable God loves to make himself known to His people.

I settled long enough for comfortable ignorance, and I wanted to know what it means to fear Him, truly fear Him, and live from that truth. I want to be a woman who lives with holy courage, devoted to a higher calling in a culture fitted for compromise. I want more than a taut ponytail, friend; I want to choose brave in my role as an image bearer in front of my children, beside my husband, before my friends, and among my community. And I have a feeling you do too.

We want to bear Christ's image with boldness. Causal Christianity isn't as comfortable as it looks because we're still living thick in fear and we know, *we know*, we were meant for more.

It all begins with fixing our eyes, unpacking our fears, and laying hold of the freedom we were created for. Here, now, today. I'm so glad you're joining me. We're better together and I'm convinced we need this.

I have heard it said that if you're going to write, you need to write about what burns like fire in your belly. I'm not sure that comment made sense to me when I first heard it. That's probably how it goes, though. We're all Helen Keller, blind to the fire, until we've felt it. We can't understand it until we've touched it, until it has touched us.

This book tells a bit of how I really began to know God and what it means to truly fear Him, in and through one of my worst fears. But even more, I pray it will propel you to find and know Him there as well. Whether those fears ever come to fruition or not, whether your prayers are answered in the way you prayed them or not, this book is about dusting off what it means to fear the Lord—yes, *fear Him*—and watching all of your other fears hang limp in the shadow of who He is. I'm convinced this is where the real fire in your belly begins. This is where choosing brave begins. Proverbs puts it this way:

> If you receive my words, and treasure my commands within you, so that you incline your ear to wisdom, and apply your heart to understanding; yes, if you cry out for discernment, and lift up your voice for understanding, if you seek her as silver, and search for her as for hidden treasures; then you will understand the fear of the LORD, and find the knowledge of God. (Proverbs 2:1–5)

We live in a world that heralds bravery, but the bravery it applauds is only a pale glimmer of the real courage, holy courage, our intimate relationship with the Creator of the universe affords. There is so much more, friend. Let's seek it, find Him, and choose brave together.

We're here, Lord Jesus, asking to know you more. Churn our hearts as we turn our eyes toward you. Be near, Jesus. Teach us. We're listening, seeking, ready to find you here. May it be so. Amen.

CHAPTER 1

The Truth about Fear

The remarkable thing about fearing God is that when you fear God you fear nothing else, whereas if you do not fear God you fear everything else.

Oswald Chambers

I lay cold on the emergency room bed and tried to answer the medic's barrage of questions. Steely instruments measured and analyzed all of me. Though I was lucid—after having passed out earlier—consciousness did not afford clarity.

"Yes, I think I am . . . was? . . . pregnant."

"No, I have not taken a pregnancy test or seen a doctor."

"No, I don't know the date of my last cycle or how far along I might be."

I was still wondering how I had arrived here. Life was normal a week ago. Now I felt like Alice tumbling down the rabbit hole, time suspended.

Either the well was very deep, or she fell very slowly, for she had plenty of time as she went down to look about her and to wonder what was going to happen next. First, she tried to look down and make out what she was coming to, but it was too dark to see anything . . .[1]

This wasn't the miscarriage story I had heard from friends. I was doing it backward—miscarrying before peeing a plus sign onto a stick. Miscarrying before making a memorable announcement to my husband. Miscarrying before my heart swelled with the earliest signs of new life. My emotions felt backward, detached, confused, and cold in a way that couldn't be touched by the warm blankets the nurse layered on me. Cold like the steely instruments they would not stop probing me with.

The ultrasound showed no sign of life; but the blood work showed the opposite. My hCG count, a noted pregnancy hormone, was abnormally high. The doctor suspected that I had either miscarried or I was showing signs of a molar pregnancy. Either way, I was stable now and there was nothing more they could do. They told me to see my ob-gyn the first chance I got and then sent me home.

It was the weekend, so we waited. I continued to pass out after major bouts of bleeding, always in the bathroom, always alone, until my husband, Ross, instated a no-closed-bathroom-door policy, which ended up becoming a you-are-not-allowed-to-go-to-the-bathroom-alone policy. I am private, borderline prudish, when it comes to bathroom doors. I like them locked. If I had any sense of decency left in me after my first pregnancy, this second pregnancy seemed likely to drain me of it quickly. But it turns out that fainting is far more frightening for the bystanding husband than it is for the wife doing the fainting. So I sheepishly followed the new rules.

I survived the weekend under surveillance, fixing my eyes on my Monday appointment. *This* would be closure. I set my heart there decidedly. When life spins out of control, we often grasp for, become appeased by, that which we *think* we can control. This Monday appointment was a finality I could sink into, lean against wearily. I was ready for it.

Ross and I sat through the protocol appointment and listened to well-rehearsed statistics. *Nearly one in four pregnancies ends in miscarriage. This happens far more frequently than you are likely aware of. It's not your fault; we often do not know why these things happen. Give yourself some time. Try again.*

I sat stiff, unable to make myself comfortable. How did I wind up here? All of these events were becoming a tangled mess in my brain. "Try again" sounds strange when you weren't trying in the first place. A few days ago I was a healthy young woman still adjusting to life as a stay-at-home mom. Now I was a sterile statistic being offered paltry encouragement. And I wondered, *How do I get back to where I was before?*

Following our brief discussion with the doctor, we waited for an ultrasound. This would be a simple check to make sure my body processed the miscarriage as expected. While we waited our turn, I exhaled for what felt like the first time in a week. I was hungry for normal, and it was near, I was certain of it.

We were checking off the final boxes to be released from this mini nightmare. I lay on the ultrasound table with my heart hanging tightly to that hope. And the screen came alive with the rhythm of a tiny heartbeat. It required no explanation. I was pregnant. Amid the bleeding and fainting, pregnant. In the middle of my weakness and fear, there was a tiny life pounding out a steady beat inside of me.

19

This wasn't normal. This wasn't expected. So with a heaping dose of caution, they sent me home. And overcome with emotions I couldn't even name or process, I finally cried.

The Reality of Fear

Fear is real. Can we establish this right here, right now? It's really real. We know this when the phone rings in the middle of the night and when an oncoming car crosses the center line as it approaches. We know this when we wake shaking from the too-real nightmare or when we hold our breath silently, waiting for a heartbeat to appear on an ultrasound screen. We might attempt to ignore our heart as it races, pretend our muscles aren't tense from the inside out. We may be able to cop a thin smile that convinces a stranger otherwise, but you and I, we know the truth. You simply can't tighten your ponytail and pretend fear away.

That doesn't mean I haven't tried. I have. Every single time Ross is gone overnight I try it. As darkness settles, the house grows quieter and louder at the same time. Nighttime noises my ears would never notice if Ross were lying next to me become unignorable. Normal dog and cat noises become someone trying to climb my second-story bedroom window. I tell myself to knock it off, that it isn't even rational. Yet no matter how bossy I get, I'm still scared. I can't talk myself out of the fear.

The *effects* of this fear are also real. My heart beats faster. My mind concocts stories and continues on with these arguments:

ME: *I'm scared.*
ALSO ME: *Knock it off, you're being silly.*
ALSO ME: *I can't sleep.*

Can I overcome this fear? Sure I can. We all go to sleep eventually, right? But denying the fear's existence is a useless waste of energy. It's fear and it's real.

Defining (and Re-Defining) Fear

But *what is fear, really*? In my earliest research I appealed to the ever-objective Merriam-Webster and was surprised by what I found there:

Definition of Fear

1: a: an unpleasant often strong emotion caused by anticipation or awareness of danger
   b: (1): an instance of this emotion
       (2): a state marked by this emotion
2: anxious concern: SOLICITUDE
3: profound reverence and awe especially toward God
4: reason for alarm: DANGER[2]

Did you catch that third definition of the word? *Profound reverence and awe especially toward God.* That is big G, capital G, God. Why does Merriam-Webster define the word with an understanding that most of us believers, who are called to live it, do not practically comprehend? We cannot afford to settle for false familiarity or modern desensitization to a word so critical to our relationship with God. We have to understand fear.

Once we establish our baseline—we believe fear is real—we must flesh out some truths about fear that can help us grasp its complexity.

Fear Affects Us Emotionally and Demands a Visceral Response

Our response to fear is involuntary. As mine does in response to those nighttime noises when my husband is away, our bodies respond innately. Our hearts race. Our breathing quickens. We cry. From our deepest core our body responds in awareness and anticipation of whatever our brain has deemed fearful.

This response is a neon sign that points us to alarm. *Red alert, red alert, this diagnosis, being up that high, taking on this financial risk, is scary.* The potential or magnanimity of what we are staring down is sending off sirens somewhere deep inside us. You know this. You have felt it.

What is fascinating, though, is how the Bible talks about fear. The Greek and Hebrew root words do not precisely differentiate between fears (something we'll discuss more in-depth in chapter 2), and neither do our emotions. Have you ever considered that?

Last summer my family camped in the Idaho panhandle near Lake Pend Oreille. As darkness blanketed the camp, we piled in the truck and drove deeper into the woods until we found a clearing. When we stepped out of the truck, we were completely engulfed in darkness. An enormous black sky pocked full of the most brilliant stars hung heavy over us. Stars were everywhere. Away from the pollution of light, these stars set the darkness on fire in a way I had never seen before—the Milky Way, constellations, and satellites all came out of obscurity for our viewing. We could not help but look up. Our captivation and joy, our wonder, and yes, even our fear, was visceral and real. We could actually feel the fear as we tried to comprehend who we are in this vast universe. *This is incredible,* I thought. *God, we are so, so small here.*

I hope you have felt these emotions when standing before pounding ocean waves, when you have held newly formed life in your hands, or when you kept a good distance from giant licks of fire. I hope you have gazed long at a tightly spun chrysalis, toed the lip of the Grand Canyon, or sat captivated as angry thunder clouds churned above you. It's not just a thought; this grandeur is felt deep. We don't create that; profound awe and fear produce it as we consider something so much greater than ourselves.

Do you see it, friend? This is why the cute social media memes telling us to be fearless don't fix anything. We can nod, like, and share all we want, but that euphoria is useless in making any real change. Our fear isn't imaginary. It demands a proper response. And it's about time we figure out one that can actually make a difference.

The Wisdom that Rightly Aligns Fear

As we move into maturity and adulthood, we begin the process of weighing our hearts against our brains, our feelings and emotions against what we know to be true. This happens in the most casual of circumstances. For example, I really want to eat a doughnut. It will taste good. I think I need it. But it is not good for me. An egg is a wiser choice for my blood sugar and waistline. This is wisdom bossing my feelings around. And let's be honest, wisdom does not always win.

Fear is much the same: it is a God-given emotion we get to guide and measure against an ever-growing (hopefully) body of wisdom. How interesting that in Proverbs we learn that the fear of the Lord is actually the *very beginning* of wisdom (see Proverbs 9:10). The *fear of the Lord* is the key to wisdom, and wisdom is key to rightly aligning our fear.

When we fill our minds with truth, we strengthen our spiritual scales, calibrating them to properly weigh our emotions.

Our decisions, reactions, and responses begin to align with the truth of what we believe rather than the undulating waves of our perceptions and emotions.

My nighttime fears when my husband is away are another good example here. I feel the fear. My body responds to that fear and I can either follow the path of my emotions, often the easy route, or force my mind to lean on what I know to be true in that situation. This is where our fear of the Lord and our fear of everything else begins to differ.

The more comfortable we get in a new situation, whether public speaking or, say, zip-lining, the more conditioned we become to fighting the fear. We become increasingly comfortable there and fear less. On the contrary, when we fear the Lord, the more we know Him (Proverbs 9:10), the more we seek and find Him, the more we study and hear and obey Him, *the more we fear Him.* The fear of the Lord causes us to move *toward* Him.

We Worship What We Fear

Fear always points us toward something. It's sneaky, not always direct, but it provides clues that point us toward the truth of what we value and what we believe. Our fears and continual stress about finances, for instance, point to our deep-seated value of security and the belief that money is our means to achieve that security.

Our stranglehold on our children, helicopter tendencies, or inability to let them grow without our continual input even as adults, speaks loudly of our need for control. Similarly, when we are the grown children of helicopter parents, our submission to their unhealthy behavior points toward our fear of them. Can you see it? Our fears point toward what we prize. Fear is always directional.

When we understand that fear is directional, we can begin to grasp that what we fear is what we worship. Worship is defined as an act of esteem or devotion, great honor, reverence, or veneration. The crossover between the definition of fear and worship is interesting and not incidental. We fear what we hold in high regard, that which is elevated in our hearts.

That is concerning for a girl like me who has sat long in the pew—a girl who has known the first of the Ten Commandments, to have no other gods before Him, for most her life; a girl who has scoffed many times at those Israelites who melted their jewelry to make a golden calf to worship. I have sat comfortably, loftily thinking I had that first commandment nailed until one quick look at my fears revealed otherwise. That's a serious checkpoint, isn't it? What are *your* fears pointing to? What are you choosing to *worship*?

Just as our limits, our weaknesses, point us to seek His aid, our fear of the Lord perfectly positions us to worship Him. Glimpsing our limits, the end of us, a lack of control or ability to make things happen, pushes up against the reality of who God is. We are created in the image of God, but we are not God, and sometimes we confuse the two. And when we do, idolatry creeps in on every front. We elevate ourselves, our control, our knowledge. We take on the *tighten your ponytail* theology and trip hard under the weight of disappointment and shame when our efforts don't produce the results we deserve in our career, in our spouse, in our kids. Fearing God, knowing and worshiping Him, grasping the magnitude of His greatness, positions us to rightly honor Him. It's no surprise we're told wisdom starts here.

This becomes our baseline, internalizing proper alignment, proper positioning before a holy God, before we ever get to choose brave. Fear is real. It demands a response. Our hearts naturally boss our brains around. Fear is directional. We will worship what we fear.

So what are we to do with this fear? What does it mean to choose brave—to pursue holy courage with godly fear? The Bible actually has a lot to say here. If you are anything like me, you have been glossing over some pretty important Scriptures for far too long. So let's engage. Let's toss the social media memes' three-step process to fighting fear. Let's forget the idea of bootstrapping our brave and say good-bye to the idea of fearlessness. Let the chaff be. Good and godly fear is at the heart of this message. You weren't called to fearlessness. You were called to fear the Lord.

Fear, my friend, might be the new brave.

CHAPTER 2

What Do I Know of Holy?

> To what will you look for help if you will not look to that which
> is stronger than yourself.
>
> C.S. Lewis, Mere Christianity

I have loved newspapers for as long as I can remember. With their inky scent and languid structure, they are an oversized Do Not Disturb sign filled with things to learn and know. Growing up a small-town girl, newspapers held the stories that would inch me beyond my small room, my small house, my small world. I read them faithfully. I even liked the ashy remains that lingered on my fingertips, evidence I had been somewhere.

I began young with the comics, the cotton-candy appetizer of *Family Circus* and *Dennis the Menace*, to which Johnny Hart added shape and weight with *B.C.* My interest only grew from there—the sports page, headlines, opinion pieces, classifieds. As I grew older, I navigated the obituaries and death notices like a crossword. In my barely-bigger-than-Mayberry[1] hometown, the names were often familiar, and life-and-death news spread by word of mouth long before the paper kid could deliver it to our door. But in the event it hadn't, I'd puzzle my own story out of the clues provided and see if I could fill in the blanks.

Some games we play are quite natural in our everyday, secluded parts of our minds, but they feel weird and creepy when we write about them later. Here is my weird and creepy. I find it entertaining to play real-life Clue with death notices.

Obits of older people made for easier guesswork—it felt detached, and older people are closer to death anyway, I believed, so it seemed natural. But I always got hung up on the babies—the death notices of the most vulnerable. Those were not games to be played, puzzles to be riddled out. Those were wholly sad and without any logical clues.

How in the world does that happen? And why? I'd wonder. *How do people survive that kind of loss?* Long before marriage and motherhood, I never wondered about the *child* lost to sudden infant death syndrome (SIDS), illness, an automobile accident; I only wondered about the parents. Even in my most egocentric teen years I could taste the slightest asphyxiation of that typeset reality: *How do people reconcile, survive the loss of the completely innocent?*

My quietly formed questions folded tidily, creased easily, like a newspaper in my heart. I tucked them away, let them rest there, never imagining I would one day live them out, cry them out, and plead with God for answers to those very whys and hows.

This is how our comfy *what if* fears often begin—in quiet, far-off places, worst-case-scenario daydreams—nightmares really—that only happen to someone else. As we age they inch closer, come to life in greater clarity. Perhaps they are *not* just the stuff of bad movies or newspapers anymore. Marriages really do dissolve. People really do lose their jobs. Houses burn down, dreams go up in smoke, and people you love can make really bad choices. With this realization and its claustrophobic proximity, we start to learn that real life can be real scary.

What's even scarier is how bereft we can be, how ill-equipped we are to actually do something about the real scary. We read of yet-another school shooting, a gunman at the local grocery story. It's close and we're almost numb. Helpless. We watch a solid family dissolve, hearts break—and if it can happen to them, we *know* it can happen to anyone. The disease diagnosis is no respecter of age, and if we pause long enough to add it up, it's hard not to feel sick and powerless in the wake of all this death and destruction. Everywhere. How does a person live in the real brokenness of this world and not feel completely frozen by fear?

This is the answer I longed for when my hope was frayed thin, when the answer to my prayer was not what I prayed for. This is the realization the Lord has patiently taught me when the newspaper story became *my story* and fear-colored lenses became my own. In and through the story I didn't want, knitted closely to seeking for the promised hope He has given us in Scripture, He has taught me more about fear and freedom and courage than I ever could have imagined.

We are not helpless or hopeless here, friend. We needn't become calloused or indifferent to the fear two steps outside our front door or the fear that has already crossed the threshold. He's given us a game plan we've assumed is outdated or stale. And dusting off this truth is going to be essential.

So let me be so forward as to ask, what is it for you? What is the fear that plays at the edges of your mind—the quiet one, the one you might not even mention to your closest friend? What is the worst-case-scenario script you've run again and again—the one that makes your stomach turn or keeps you up at night? What is igniting your fear, the thing you desperately need to face with courage? What are those imaginative questions and circumstances framed in by realities and folded neatly into your subconscious mind that threaten to rob your sanity, your peace? You may have deep-seated fears whose presence you barely even notice. They grow quietly in shadowy recesses, a crumpled doormat you keep tripping over rather than addressing. But you have given them an address and jurisdiction that swells into your reality days, weeks, and sometimes even years later.

There's a better way. The Bible commands it and it has been right in front of you all along. What if you could take hold of it? Would you chase after it? The fear of the Lord is that kind of invitation, that kind of game-changer, friend.

What Does It Even Mean to Fear God?

It was a simple idea. I author a blog called I Choose Brave, with the tagline *Fear God. Live Brave.* And I wanted to *really know* that title, unpack it in my own study. I wanted to track Scriptures on the topic and read them all in context, because that is what good Bible study girls do, right?

I Choose Brave. I Fear God. I Live Brave. I would press on until I thoroughly understood it.

But what I began to uncover was more than a simple word study, more complex and adventurous than a rabbit trail. What I unearthed would lay me bare, expose my own hidden and unprocessed fears, run amok in ways that I barely knew, and position me to understand fear in a whole new way.

When I was a kid, somewhere between church and Christian school, I adopted a watered-down view of what it means to fear God. Without even realizing, I had done far more than water it down; I had soaked and saturated the whole concept until the Word lay in my hands like a limp paper towel.

Sure the Bible says that, I told myself. *But that's not what it really means. It doesn't mean* fear *in the traditional sense. It means respect. We respect God. Like our elders. Like the flag. So of course we respect Him, because He's God. The end.*

Wrap that thing up, neat and tidy. Done. I accepted the answer without further pause and adopted it quietly for decades.

Sure, I'd heard or read verses that talked about fearing God. Verses like:

> You have given a banner to those who fear You, that it may be displayed because of the truth. (Psalm 60:4)

> The fear of the Lord is a fountain of life, to turn one away from the snares of death. (Proverbs 14:27)

> Men and brethren, sons of the family of Abraham, and those among you who fear God, to you the word of this salvation has been sent. (Acts 13:26)

I didn't really need to process these verses. I knew they were there, *mostly.* I understood them as much as I felt I needed to, and placed them on a neat little shelf in my heart. And I thought, *No, of course we don't fear a kind, gentle Creator. God is love. We respect Him.*

But the first time I committed to reading the entire Bible in a year, drinking in Scripture at a more rapid rate, I noticed this commission, this call to fear Him *over and over again.* Like, a whole lot. We're commanded to fear the Lord nearly as much as we're told *not* to fear. It forced me to stop and really consider the whole idea.

What is that all about? I thought. *It must be kind of important, right? Why don't we hear much about this?* The more I studied God's Word, the more I wondered. Maybe there was more to fearing God than I realized. I began to ask myself serious questions:

What *does* it mean to fear God?
What kind of fear is that? Are there different varieties of fear?
Why is *this* fear threaded through Scripture so frequently and yet no one seems to talk about it?
How do I understand fear and at the same time not understand it at all?
And how in the world could fear really give us courage, give us freedom, and afford us peace?

These aren't simple questions, but they're definitely worth digging into, don't you think? Do me a favor and lay aside your childhood or otherwise-adopted definition of the fear of the Lord for a minute, let's wander through Scripture together, and consider with me what fearing God looks like in some of the stories that have shaped our faith:

Moses

From the burning bush God spoke to Moses saying:

"I am the God of your father—the God of Abraham, the God of Isaac, and the God of Jacob." And Moses hid his face for he was afraid to look upon God. (Exodus 3:6)

Joshua

When the Commander of the army of the Lord met Joshua, he said:

"As Commander of the army of the LORD I have now come." And Joshua fell on his face to the earth and worshiped, and said to Him, "What does my Lord say to His servant?" (Joshua 5:14).

Isaiah

In the year that King Uzziah died, I saw the Lord sitting on a throne, high and lifted up, and the train of His robe filled the temple. Above it stood seraphim; each one had six wings: with two he covered his face . . . (Isaiah 6:1–2)

The picture Isaiah paints is incredible and worth continuing, but I want to stop here and capture what the seraphim are doing. Beyond crying out, "Holy, holy, holy, is the LORD of hosts; the whole earth is full of His glory!"[2] at a decibel that causes the very doorposts to tremble, a volume you can feel, the seraphim—these holy and perfect beings standing just above Him—are *covering their faces in the presence of God.*

Isaiah is completely undone in His presence and yet boldly leans in and finds his voice: "Here am I! Send me."[3]

Do you see the balance of the fear and glory, the grace and courage to step into, fall facedown before, all that is holy? The reactions of these men were deep, almost involuntary, and completely unheard of today.

My long-owned definition of fear seems both weak and dull here. *Respect?* Is that what these men were experiencing—some good old-fashioned respect? I can't make that work. Something is off.

It was in this digging that I began to realize for the first time that I had no idea what was going on here. Like the Addison Road song of the same name, the question reverberated deep—*What do I know of holy?* The answer sounded weakly like nothing, nothing at all.

I know what fear is in my daily life. I felt it in the second grade when Mrs. West called on me and I didn't know the answer. Or that hollow, sinking feeling the time I lost my lunch tickets. I felt fear when my mom delayed discipline with, "We'll talk about this when your father gets home." That fear rippled through my little body quick.

Fear and I have had this on-and-off-again relationship through most of life—the self-conscious teen years and launching twenties, my years as a clueless new bride (yes, that can last for a few years) and with a fresh anointing in motherhood. You could say fear and I are well acquainted.

But what does that ugly fear have to do with this *God* fear? They seemed miles apart in my mind, but were they? My early excavation of the Word was surprising to me. The Greek and Hebrew roots used for fear in the Bible weren't all that helpful. That's not entirely true. Of course they were helpful, but not in the way I was hoping.

You see, in my mind, looking up the root words for *fear* would be like the root words for *love*. I still remember learning the three Greek words for *love* back in Sunday school—*philos*, *eros*, and *agape*. I intended to dig up the root words for fear, sort them out, and voilà! In nice and tidy categories, there we'd have it—good fear, bad fear, do not fear, do fear. God fear, Katie fear.

I figured I would be able to puzzle this thing out quite easily. Except, it didn't quite work that way.

I started with the Greek word *phobeo*, used for fear throughout much of the New Testament. In Matthew 10:28, for instance, it shows up in red letters—which is to say, they are Jesus' words:

Do not fear [phobeo] those who kill the body but cannot kill the soul. But rather fear [phobeo] Him who is able to destroy both soul and body in hell.

A light verse, no? But the meaning here is clear that we are talking about fear of the Lord—what I might have previously understood, in a limp-paper-towel sort of way, as respect.

A few chapters later in Matthew 14:5 we find a hotheaded Herod showing the same fear, the same phobeo. Herod was angry at John the Baptist for condemning Herod's hookup with his own sister-in-law. So angry, in fact, he wanted to kill him.

The Scripture tells us, "Although he wanted to put him to death, he feared [phobeo] the multitude, because they counted him as a prophet."

Do you see the rub here? This phobeo isn't the holy fear we were talking about in Matthew 10. This is scared-everyone-is-going-to-be-mad-at-me, scared-of-a-riot fear. There isn't much holy about Herod or his fear here.

And that is where understanding fear gets tricky and begins to mess with every preconceived notion I had. Fear is fear. The word is one and the same—the good ones, the bad ones, the ones I (think I) understand, the ones that are fuzzy, and the ones I have spent years tucking away like inky newspapers in my heart—unpacking the fear of the Lord, this fear that I believe affords freedom and bravery, wasn't going to be quite as easy as I thought.

I began to pray:

What do I know of holy, God? What does it mean to fear you and live brave? I know this matters because this mix of emotions is more real than ever to me. I see it written all over your Word, Lord, and I feel real fear in my everyday life. I try to summon courage from my own strength, but it is empty, shallow, hollow.

The challenges of this world are real. The kids we are raising and these parents that are aging, it's bringing us to our knees, God, and it's scary. The threats to our marriages are more vile, more insipid than we've ever seen, and it's scary. Gunmen are in our schools, in our neighborhoods, in our churches. It's all so close and all so real, God. The stakes are high. I long for us to be a generation that seeks your name, but there is so much to fear. Where do we even begin?

Perhaps that's a prayer you pray too?

God says He grants wisdom to those who ask (see James 1:5). Could it be that simple? That He wants us to take Him at His Word, to ask, to seek, and to trust to find Him on the other side of our questions, in, through, and *about* our fear?

I believe it is that simple, friend. And when we're done, I pray that we'll walk away with inky remains of His Word on our hearts, pulsing in our veins. That we'll see Him anew, relate to Him with a fresh fervor, clearly understand a holy fear that changes us, compels our courage in the here and now. Real evidence that we have been somewhere. We're stepping in that direction, bravely. Pause and join me?

O God, we seek to know you more here. Speak. Teach. Lead. By your Holy Spirit, open our ears and eyes, prompt our hearts, help us pay attention to you, help us understand what holy is. Lift our gaze, drown our misinterpretations and misunderstandings, the cultural and collective noise. We want to know you more. God, teach us what it means to fear you, what it means to step out in holy courage. We come ready and willing. Be all. Leave us changed. Amen.

CHAPTER 3

When Life Gets your Attention

It is the ability to choose which makes us human.

Madeleine L'Engle, Walking on Water:
Reflections on Art & Faith

There are some moments that change our lives and we don't even know it. At least not *in that moment*. Some days are impregnated with change, so expected or overdue we can see it coming a mile away. We move, get married, birth a child, or take our first shaky step down a new career path. But other life-changing moments show up quietly, quickly, by surprise even, and somehow our cones and rods need hindsight to identify their magnitude.

The world around us looks, feels, and tastes different now. *Oh, that was the day*, we think.

For me, *this* was the day.

I was twenty-five years old, a new mama, when I started bleeding unexpectedly two weeks after my first postpartum cycle. It seemed odd but not overly worrisome. Maybe my body was having a false start getting into the swing of things again.

My firstborn, Tyler, was nine months old now. All the wild ways motherhood would impact (is still impacting?) my body were new to me. But life had swung at a pretty steady pace thus far.

At twenty-one I married the boy I cheered for on the high school basketball team. We had decent jobs, renovated a charming home, and waited a few years before starting a family. Mostly our plans seemed to work on demand. Nine months after we decided we were ready, we had a healthy baby boy. Nine more months and my body was now trying to figure out a steady rhythm again, I supposed.

When the bleeding didn't stop after a few days, fear began to creep in. I couldn't shrug it off any longer and I called a nurse at my doctor's office. She asked if I could be pregnant—it was possible I was having a miscarriage. She told me there wasn't much we could do at this point besides wait and see how my body responded. Her words seemed overzealous and foreign. Pregnant? A miscarriage? It felt like being told I might need a root canal on a tooth that never hurt. *A what?*

Even so, I called a friend who had experienced a miscarriage and asked for all the details. This is how we learn, right? Toeing in new territory, we spot someone who has been there and listen closely to every detail. They all matter now.

Armed with some borrowed experiential wisdom and very little knowledge of my own, I approached this slightly concerning bump in the road with the only boot-strapping voracity I knew: *Whatever this is, keep your head down and your chin up; you can get through this. Dig deep.* You know, tighten your ponytail and move along.

A few days later, shortly after going to bed, I woke up and everything was wrong. I was sticky and wet, the epicenter of blood-soaked sheets. I woke my husband, Ross, and told him I needed help. What kind of help, I didn't know, but something was wrong.

In a sleepy stupor I stumbled to the bathroom. The world felt animated, warm, soft, and slow. The temperature seemed to be rising quickly and I decided if I pressed my face to the cool bathroom counter for just a minute I would feel better. Confusion is interesting and often unrecognizable when you're in it. The next thing I remember was my body flat, comfortable, on the hard bathroom floor. Ross was panicked, standing beside me, and Tyler cried from his crib in the neighboring room.

My world was still warm and dreamy and I was incapable of adopting any of Ross's urgency. He told me the paramedics were on their way, and I begged him to walk me back to our bedroom, where I curled up in the fetal position against the wall, dressed in only a T-shirt and underwear. The small part of my brain that was properly functioning knew something was wrong. People were coming to my house, and I wanted pants. I needed pants. But fear and confusion left me paralyzed.

Have you been here, friend? The phone call comes, the news drops, and it absolutely sucks the air from your lungs. In a moment everything changes and no matter how hard your brain tries, it can't seem to reconcile everything. Simple tasks become mountains as fear becomes infectious, eating away at your ability to process. The challenge before you consumes your thoughts, you size it up from every angle, stare at it dazed, and yet are incapacitated to do anything about it.

It's completely foreign and yet, in a way, normal. Because when life takes an abrupt turn, grabs our attention, we are caught off balance. It's scary. And what we choose to do here matters more than we even know.

The Invitation

In Exodus 3 we meet Moses in the desert near Horeb, and God is about to get his attention. Moses' turn-and-look moment is at first a little more subtle—he didn't pass out on the bathroom floor, get a stomach-turning phone call, but life was about to get his attention just the same. I love the simplicity with which we are introduced to his story in Scripture.

> Moses thought, "I will go over and see this strange sight—why the bush does not burn up" (Exodus 3:3 NIV).

Plain and simple, right? But the previous verse tells us the Angel of the Lord was appearing in a flame of fire from this bush. This is a *really big deal*. A big deal, which is completely not reflected in the casualness of Moses' thoughts. It makes me think he doesn't fully understand what's in front of him yet. Isn't that just so relatable? Life changes abruptly, wildly, smack in the ordinary threads of our every day and we don't even see it coming. We've been there, Moses. We get you.

Scripture gives us Moses' backstory in pretty great detail—his baby-basket rescue by Pharaoh's daughter after his mother floated him down the Nile River to escape certain death, growing up in Pharaoh's palace as an heir, and murdering an Egyptian—all before we meet him tending sheep for a solid forty years in the desert of Midian. Here he catches sight of a random bush burning wildly. He stares as the hungry flames dance and utters that most simplistic sentence: "I will go over and see this strange sight—why the bush does not burn up."

Can you see his simple, conscious decision? A man, faithful in his work—work well below his status and experience, education, and training—is bossing himself around, telling himself to turn aside from his "normal" and go see what is going on.

He could have ignored this burning bush, because it clearly wasn't going to cause much of an issue there in the desert, but his curiosity was piqued. A bush that does not burn up. His heart was prompted. He chose to move toward it. And it was at this moment, *in his choosing to pursue, to step toward*, that God spoke.

> When the LORD saw that he turned aside to look, God called to him from the midst of the bush and said, "Moses, Moses!" . . .
>
> Then He said, "Do not draw near this place. Take your sandals off your feet, for the place where you stand is holy ground."
>
> Moreover He said, "I am the God of your father—the God of Abraham, the God of Isaac, and the God of Jacob." And Moses hid his face, for he was afraid to look upon God. (Exodus 3:4–6)

This entire story, one many of us heard first around Sunday school tables with felt-board cutouts of a gray-haired and bearded Moses standing near a cute bush with a cozy fire beckoning marshmallows, Hershey bars, and graham crackers, takes on new meaning when we meet it with maturity.

The fire's appetite was insatiable. It just kept burning. I imagine the singeing briars stung Moses' nostrils, he could taste them even, as he made the conscious decision to pause with curiosity, to turn, to see, to move forward.

But what drew him was not what kept him there. In the same manner, what draws us to God—curiosity, interest, wonder—is not what keeps us there.

Moses was not scared in his approach; fear came when he realized the presence of God in those most casual coordinates. Right there in the middle of the desert on a normal day, fear came when he realized he was standing in the presence of the almighty God.

Do not draw near. Take off your shoes. It came as a command, not a request. And while the cultural implications of this statement have been touted by scholars far and wide, I wonder if there is even more to it than respect and tradition, even more than just a command. Could this be an invitation?

I am here, God seemed to say. *Feel my presence. In this place, remove the barrier that separates, that protects, that hides your humble and rugged feet, and touch the ground that I am pervading. I am huge, so much bigger than you can grasp and imagine, Moses. Feel me, fear me.*

Can we even begin to grasp that—a God who is *that mighty,* who is *that powerful,* inhabiting an insatiable fire and yet beckons us nearer in submission, draws us closer still?

It was in this moment that Moses hid his face. Amid an invitation to submission, to the purest veneration of a holy God, he was afraid.

God proceeded to tell Moses that He had seen and heard the bondage and tears of the Israelites. And in Exodus 3:10 we read the words that make the fear of the Lord different from any other: "Come now, therefore, and I will send you . . ." *The fear of God is a fear that bids us to come.*

While every other fear you experience is pushing you away from what scares you, the fear of the Lord invites you *into* His presence, *into* His work, *into* intimacy and nearness with the God who breathes stars. That's a wild invitation.

I know what you're thinking. Moses had it easy, right? If you were hanging out, doing your job, managing your daily gig of herding sheep or kids or laundry and groceries, you'd stop for a burning bush too. I get that, but while Moses' story is unique, his response in the presence of God is not. Let's skip forward a few books and watch Joshua's response in a completely different situation.

After Moses died, God called Joshua to lead the Israelites into the promised land. Jericho was the first city in their path. Just after crossing the Jordan River, we find Joshua, his feet fresh on a new land with the enormous task of conquering the inhabitants before him:

> It came to pass, when Joshua was by Jericho, that he lifted his eyes and looked, and behold, a Man stood opposite him with His sword drawn in His hand. (Joshua 5:13)

Isn't this a welcome greeting? Joshua is green in leading this wily and whiny group of people. He has known his calling is to battle, but his feet are barely out of the Jordan, on foreign soil, when he encounters a man standing with his sword drawn. Joshua's response here is vital.

> Joshua went to Him and said to Him, "Are you for us or for our adversaries?" (Joshua 5:13).

Can you imagine? An unknown man before him, standing on guard with his sword in hand, and Joshua moves forward in curiosity and asks, "Are we friends or enemies?"

> "Neither," he replied, "but as commander of the army of the LORD I have now come." Then Joshua fell facedown to the ground in reverence, and asked him, "What message does my

Lord have for his servant?" The commander of the Lord's army replied, "Take off your sandals, for the place where you are standing is holy." And Joshua did so. (Joshua 5:14–15 NIV)

Sound familiar? Joshua moved forward without fear. He leaned into curiosity and God spoke. At the realization of whom he was speaking to, *fear came.* He fell on his face in worship. And just as Moses was, he was commanded to take off his shoes, invited into submission, ushered into the presence of the very real God pulsing holiness into the earth around him.

There is a pattern here I don't want us to miss. A pattern beyond the lines we have heard so many times and memorized into triviality. *God is moving in and amid the everyday calling of people who are following hard after Him.*

He enters and engages in unique ways, and those wildly after His heart press in, nearer. They pause and move toward His unique engagement. They lean in with curiosity. And when God speaks, when He invites them in intimately, they are overcome with a fear like no other.

Tell me the last time you fell facedown in awe of what was before you. When was the last time you hid your face for fear of the greatness you were beholding? These are brave men we are talking about. Men who have known difficulty and battle, men who were trained and skilled and learned and yet were trembling and hiding, wholly consumed by all that is holy.

This isn't "respect." You and I both know that. This is what it means to be consumed by the power of our very real God, to enter one tiny step into His presence, to feel the earth teeming with His greatness. Facedown, hiding.

This is veneration, overcome with awe toward the One to whom we have granted full authority and authorship of our lives. This is fear, stirring and trembling in the presence of One so incredibly greater than us. And in the midst of our normal and everyday life-changing moments we may have planned for or never even saw coming, we get to choose to move toward it, to move toward Him.

Let that sink in a bit. God does not need our respect. Let's toss that watered-down definition of fear out the window because we are dealing with something entirely different here.

You may find yourself wandering casually in the desert, just doing your job, or curled up on your bedroom floor with paramedics on the way. The attention-getting scenario may be abrupt or more subtle. But the invitation is the same either way. We are invited to submission in the midst of it. We are invited into holy worship, pure veneration of the only One worthy of our fear.

Take off your shoes. Walk barefoot, moving forward onto the holy ground that permeates your life, pursuing what He is igniting in you. He wants to use it all—your history, your present, your future, your huge life-changing moments, and the quieter ones that may appear in the ministry of our every day. Step forward in courage, believing He will teach you to see Him anew and to fear Him, and Him alone, right in the midst of the very thing you fear.

CHAPTER 4

Good-Bye Fearlessness

Unless we are profoundly certain God is our Father, we will
never be able to say "Thy will be done."

Timothy Keller, Prayer: Experiencing Awe
and Intimacy with God

"Guess what? I'm pregnant!" The phone calls I made on my way home from the doctor's appointment were some of my favorite calls ever. Even more fun than the time I told my mom I was pregnant with our firstborn. We were heading out the door to dinner, and in her surprise, my mom let her purse slide right off her shoulder and crash to the floor. You can't fake purse-dropping surprise.

And yet, after a tough few days of bleeding and fainting, here we were again. No one was expecting this. We were having a baby.

The doctor sent us home with a heaping dose of caution; things did not look right. The amniotic sac cocooning this tiny new life was ragged, misshapen, possibly torn. Heaping doses of caution have never been my specialty, though. I prefer hope and excitement. I do patience and caution like a kid waiting for Christmas. But my body was not about to let me forget the real state of things. It never let up.

The blood came again in wild surges, a surprise visitor who never called ahead—predictably unpredictable. My doctor warned us this might happen and instructed us not to bother calling when it did. "Just get here fast," she advised. And so we did—my car seat covered with old bath towels. My husband driving to save a life, we made the forty-five-minute drive from our tiny town in record time. More talking. More caution. Another ultrasound. We still had a baby.

And this became our lives for the next few weeks. Blood gushed, we rushed, and a little heartbeat met us on the screen every time. I didn't know how this could possibly become our new normal, but it did. The bleeding eventually slowed, and with it, the state of emergency, but the impact of my unstable state changed everything.

While not prescribed complete bed rest, the heavy dose of caution now blanketed not just the baby, but my entire life. The link between my physical activity and what they medically termed "sub-chronic bleeding" was sketchy at best, but why take any unnecessary risks? My need for control gnawed at me constantly, as did the fear of potential guilt. I was the incubator for this fragile life. What if something I did—past, present, or future—further compromised the baby? Dissect that one for a minute. Not only do we fear bad things happening, we fear being the reason or even just the potential reason they do. Do you see how this fear disease spreads vast and wild? It's pervasive, insidious.

Friends and family walked with me. I had as much support as I could possibly hope for in the form of meals and prayers and people willing to entertain my one-year-old, but there were places that support could not reach. I was the only one carrying the baby I may never hold. Life and death felt inextricably linked to me.

I became a prisoner in my own body as I feared anything that might compromise the fragile life inside of me. I feared being the reason that something went wrong. I feared going out in public because these massive bleeds paid no attention to time and space or the protection I wore. I read Scripture and wrote Scripture. I prayed and was prayed for. I reached long and hard for a fearlessness that was only a heat wave in the desert, a mirage. I couldn't pretend the facts away. I was scared. And this fear would become the seedling of the long and slow work He was doing not inside my womb, but inside my heart. I didn't know it at the time, but facing real and scary things would become the impetus for me to learn what it means to fear the Lord, what it means to live with holy courage.

My story may seem unique to you. And yet I hope you can see through that facade. It isn't. These turn-and-look moments are fertile ground for growing in faith, growing in *fear*. In a hundred different ways you've been there too—when the real world, your real life, meets this idea of fearlessness you've been sold, casually convinced of. When the weight of this broken world infringes on your comfortable Christianity and that flimsy fearlessness doesn't hold water because it's scary. It is. But we have a choice here. And fearlessness isn't it.

Hello, Fear

Walk down the home-decor aisle of Hobby Lobby or any other crafty home decor store and you're likely to find the familiar word etched in some hand-lettered font—*fearless*. It has a nice ring to it—stirs something almost instinctive in us. *Yes, I want that*. Maybe not the sign, exactly, but the moniker, the title. I wanted to live free of the fear that surged wild every time an ultrasound doppler touched my bulging belly.

We want to be free of the fear that we aren't doing enough to raise the kids we have, that God somehow picked the wrong girl for the job. We want freedom from the fear that makes us feel small and unworthy compared to every other woman who has her act together, the fear that diseases friendships, stymies our ability to dream—the fears that stagnate growth and leave us wondering what all the other women are thinking, why it's easier for everyone else. In modern terms we might call it the fear that keeps us from living our *best life*. Yes, please, sign me up for that brand of fearlessness. You too?

You'll find the same theme headlining women's conferences around the country and preached from the pulpit frequently. Because why wouldn't we want to be fearless? In the church, the concept almost always leans hard on the biblical command not to fear, coupled with the courage we see sprinkled in biblical heroes like Joshua and David. We've all heard it, right? The Bible says "Do not fear" 365 times, one for every day of the year. *Is that even true? Has anyone ever counted?*

My questions are beside the point. The commands throughout Scripture instructing us not to fear are real and true. Plenty has been written about that point. But what are we to do with the passages that actually call us *to* fear? Passages such as:

Teach me your way, O LORD, that I may walk in your truth; unite my heart to fear your name. (Psalm 86:11 ESV)

Let us hear the conclusion of the whole matter: Fear God and keep His commandments, for this is man's all. (Ecclesiastes 12:13)

His mercy is on those who fear Him from generation to generation. (Luke 1:50)

The command not to fear a variety of things is apparent throughout Scripture, but are the directives on what we are *to fear* any less pertinent? How have we come to focus so narrowly on one at the expense of the other?

Fearlessness is not the answer, friend. The message of the gospel is not the obliteration of fear but rather the proper alignment of it. We are called to fear the only One worthy—God. In Matthew 14, as Peter walked on the water, he had to keep his eyes fixed on Jesus, he had to be captivated and consumed with his Savior more than the very real and scary things going on around him. That's an important picture for us.

We find another great example woven in the accounts of Jesus sleeping on the boat in the storm. The storm was wild, even for the experienced fishermen aboard. Luke 8:23 says they were in "jeopardy" or "real danger."[1] So the situation was legit. This wasn't Katie imagining sounds outside her second-story bedroom window when her husband is away. This was a water-swamping, wind-thrashing, *I have spent much of my life on a boat but I've never seen it this bad, we're-all-gonna-die* kind of situation. Try and put yourself there for a minute. It's ugly.

In their life-or-death moment, the actions of the disciples were key. They went to Jesus, who was sleeping—*I mean, really, can you even imagine?* This is awesome. Could there possibly be a greater contrast between the very real insanity that was about to strangle this boat and the Savior who was so at peace that He was . . . asleep? Hang on tight to that, friend. That truth will serve you well. But let's keep following the story.

The disciples made their case to Jesus in no uncertain terms. "Master, Master," the Christian Standard Bible reads, "We are going to die!" This wasn't even a cry for help. It wasn't a question. These were tenured seafarers relaying the facts as they saw them. "We thought we'd wake you up and let you know," they told him in their expert opinions. "It's over. We are done!"

Without a word to His desperate disciples, Jesus awoke, rose, and rebuked the wind and the waves. In an instant the world around them was as peaceful as the sleeping Jesus had been just seconds before. Imagine the utter quiet, the perfect stillness, the holy calm as the disciples' hearts were still trembling, pumping aftershocks throughout their bodies.

Now this is where I want you to pull up a chair and park. Lean in close and listen.

Jesus then turned to face the disciples and cut deep into the silence. "Where is your faith?" He asked them.

I can feel the lump in their throats. They knew better. Didn't they know *Him*? They had sat front-row as Jesus healed Peter's mother-in-law and cleansed a leper. They had seen Him cast out spirits and listened to parable after parable straight from His lips. But their world got rocked and they were ready to go down with the ship. *Where is your faith?*

The response here is everything: "And they were afraid" (Luke 8:25).

All through that world-rocking storm, the squall posing a very real threat to their lives, neither Mark nor Luke specifically mention the disciples being afraid. Isn't that fascinating? I tend to read that into the story because it makes sense, but it's not there. That's not what the author is telling us. In both accounts, fear never entered the story until *after* the miracle.

> They feared exceedingly, and said to one another, "Who can this be, that even the wind and the sea obey him!" (Mark 4:41)

Let's bring this back to fearlessness. Were the disciples ever fearless in this story? Is this a story about their focus, how they ran to Jesus, desperate, and became fearless? Not even close. They ran to Jesus, saw His compassion and power on display, and *then* Mark mentions their fear.

In the moment that Jesus displayed His power and extinguished the storm with a few simple words, their fear turned aright, reoriented, recalibrated. It did not evaporate or dissolve like the wind and the waves; I believe it actually increased. The New King James version says in Mark 4, in that moment they feared *exceedingly*—meaning supremely, extremely, immensely—at the sight of His power.

Delivered from the storm, the disciples were not fearless, they were actually fear-*full*. Their fear didn't lessen, it moved—from the horizontal to the vertical. It went from what might take their lives to the One who would give His life for theirs. Do you see that? Instead of fearing the storm, aware of who He really was (and is), they feared the Lord.

This is the recipe, friend, not the abdication of fear but the proper positioning of it. This is what it is to know God. This is what it is to seek Him in the real and scary. To touch the edges of His garment and to lift our eyes from the horror in front of us to the God who goes before us, hemming us in from every side. This is what it is to seek peace, to find God, and to fear Him.

We often fail to notice the model of godly fear we have been given in Jesus Christ. In the garden of Gethsemane, preparing to drink the cup of suffering, the heinous death our sin would require, we read that Jesus sweat drops of blood in prayer as He carried out the Father's plan for our redemption. We know that, right? But the book of Hebrews tells us that His prayers in the garden were heard "*because* of His godly fear."[2]

What? Even Jesus? Yes, even Jesus. That Jesus sleeping through the storm, that Jesus learning obedience by the things He suffered, chose to fear God.

Fully man, fully God, Jesus chose the cross, chose us, chose obedience, chose fear. Theologian Matthew Henry explained it this way:

> Christ was heard in that he feared. . . . He had an awful sense of the wrath of God, of the weight of sin. His human nature was ready to sink under the heavy load, and would have sunk, had he been quite forsaken in point of help and comfort from God; but he was heard in this, he was supported under the agonies of death. He was carried through death; and there is no real deliverance from death but to be carried well through it.[3]

That hefty passage about knocked me over the first time I read it. Fully man, He feared vertically. Of course He did. By the grace of God He was carried through death. Of course He was. And in that suffering He learned obedience. Oh, image bearer, this is our call. Of course it is. This is exactly what Paul was talking about in Philippians 2:5 when he said to have the mind of Christ—humble, fearing, heard. Jesus learned obedience and walked that out all the way to the cross. And because of that,

> God elevated him to the place of highest honor and gave him the name above all other names, that at the name of Jesus every knee should bow, in heaven and on earth and under the earth, and every tongue confess that Jesus Christ is Lord, to the glory of God the Father. (Philippians 2:9–11 NLT)

What a Savior. What a salvation. And Paul rounds that powerful passage out with a call for us: "As you have always obeyed—not only in my presence, but now much more in my absence—continue to work out your salvation with fear and trembling" (Philippians 2:12 NIV).

Not, "Don't fear." Not, "Now go be fearless." But do as Christ did, grow in Christlikeness, let this mind be in you.

We do an unfathomable disservice to the gospel of Jesus Christ when we make our freedom, our courage, our perceived fearlessness about anything less than His blood-bought work at the cross. And when we stare that down, when we pause long enough to realize the depths of our depravity and the wild measure of His grace extended to us, yes, it will obliterate our horizontal fear. It will give shape and perspective to all we fear here, but a new fear takes over.

Behold Your God

Buying a cute hand-lettered sign, which stirs within us something deep, can't touch this. The world's brand of fearlessness is only a shade left of agnosticism here, friend. We don't need to talk ourselves out of fear, we need to reorient our fear. Like the disciples on that boat. We need to take our eyes off the fear around us. Like me in a high-risk pregnancy, we need to take our eyes off the fear inside us and we need to lock eyes with the Savior going before us in perfect peace, carrying us through this real and wild storm.

Be still. You have seen Him work. You know who He is. *Where is your faith?*

Forsake the chase for fearlessness, friend. Let's trade that in for eyes fixed on the only One worthy of our fear.

CHAPTER 5

Someone Worth Fearing

This is one of the blessings of fearing the Lord . . . [w]hen a heart is being filled with the greatness of God, there is less room for the question, "What are people going to think of me?"

Edward T. Welch, When People Are Big and God Is Small

I have lived in the city my entire life until just a few years ago. My husband finds that statement laughable, as "city" life for me has been rural and small—mostly towns in which I can count stoplights on a single hand. Even so, I was born and bred in the city limits.

A decade ago my husband and I purchased a few acres of land in hopes of one day building a home where the kids and the antelope play. More like kids, dogs, and a few chickens, but you get the point. And now we're here, with kids and space, and just the other day I watched my two youngest enjoy one of their favorite wild and free pastimes.

The cherry trees rooted two hundred feet from our front door are the regular resting place for flocks of tweety birds. With eager anticipation, I watch these two youngest birds of my own burst out the door together like wild little vultures and giggle as their uncanny approach frightens the entire flock into flight. Just like that, the sky is a web of tiny black wings, all in formation, and Bo and Brooklyn feel like proud conductors of it all.

Eyeing a magpie on the back deck that same day, Tyler, my oldest, paid close attention as another magpie decided to join the party. The second bird flew in fast, too fast almost, yet landed gracefully. "It's funny, Mom," Tyler told me, "that the kids can scare a whole flock of birds a couple hundred feet away with their little screams, but that magpie didn't even flinch when another magpie flew directly for him at about fifty miles per hour."

Interesting observation. Clearly, those birds know what's worth fearing.

Chained to fear in that abnormal pregnancy years ago, I could stand to learn from those birds. Gnawing fear I had never in my life felt before, rooted itself deep and became my hunger to control moments and outcomes. In my instinct to protect and right all that was going wrong, I focused my attention on the tragedy in front of me, inside of me, rather than the God who goes before me.

Seeing that you've lived long enough to learn how to read this book, it's fair to assume you have been there too on some level. Those phone calls or texts, the diagnoses that take your breath away. Words crash like glass and shatter, and your instinct is to fix, to control, to do something because you're scared and somehow you believe that scary situations can be remedied with more of *you*. *I will be Neosporin and a Band-Aid. I will be preventative care and respite care. I can fix whatever I fear with a fine-tuned version of* me. This isn't a new idea. We left Moses at the burning bush in chapter 2, but let's go back and find him in Exodus 3. His calling is one of my favorites. It isn't quite as impressive as Isaiah's calling in Isaiah 6, but I find something gritty (read: blind and distracted) about Moses that I resonate with. Pay attention to the first-person pronouns and attached verbs in this passage; I've italicized them for your benefit here:

The Lord said: "*I have* surely seen the oppression of *My* people who are in Egypt, and have heard their cry because of their taskmasters, for *I know* their sorrows. So *I have* come down to deliver them out of the hand of the Egyptians, and to bring them up from the land to a good and large land, to a land flowing with milk and honey, to the place of the Canaanites and the Hittites and the Amorites and the Perizzites and the Hivites and the Jebusites. Now therefore, behold, the cry of the children of Israel has come to *Me*, and *I have* also seen the oppression with which the Egyptians oppress them. Come now, therefore, and *I will send* you to Pharaoh that you may bring *My* people, the children of Israel out of Egypt" (Exodus 3:7–10).

God is making a point here in no uncertain terms. Scan back over those pronouns—better yet, pause and underline them in your own Bible. He has seen, He knows, these are His people, and by His power and strength and knowledge He is sending Moses to Egypt. And Moses' response here would be laughable if it weren't so familiar.

But Moses said to God, "Who am *I* that *I* should go to Pharaoh, and that *I* should bring the children of Israel out of Egypt?" (v. 11)

Don't miss that contrast, friend. God shows up and says, "Moses, this is who I am and this is what I am going to do," and Moses shoots back like a teenager with selective hearing, "Right. Yeah. So what about me, God?"

Do you see where Moses' eyes, and thus his heart, are focused? Rather than being fixed on the God pulsing through the earth below him, burning wild in the bush in front of him, he is consumed by the fear inside of him—eyes locked on all he doesn't know.

The dialogue does not stop there. Read on in chapter 3 and chapter 4 and you'll find this back-and-forth, again funny if it weren't familiar, where God says, "This is who I am and what I am going to do." And Moses shoots back a laundry list of reasons why this is a bad idea.

In his book *Awe*, Paul David Tripp boils down Moses' reactions perfectly: "It's as if the fear of personal inadequacy and political danger blinded his eyes to the awesome glory of the One sending him. Moses is not in awe of God. No, the awe capacity of his heart has been captured by fear of the Egyptians, and all he can think of is being released from the task which God has appointed him."[1]

I get it, Moses. I promise I do. You too?

Muscle Memory

The other day I drove the country roads leading to our home with my youngest daughter, Brooklyn. Night had fallen, the air was thick with fog, and the sparse light from the occasional houses was marshmallowy, distorted.

"Mama?" my girl called from the back seat. "How do you know where we are?"

"Well . . . I kind of don't," I replied. Honest but not exactly reassuring words to hand an eight-year-old feeling uncertain of her ghostly surroundings. But it was true. My eyes darted for recognition just as hers did, and I couldn't piece much of my surroundings together. I wasn't sure which road was coming next, which houses belonged to which families, or even how soon the next stop sign was approaching. I was blind on the road I've driven for years, trusting it would get me where I was going and that I would know when to turn when I got there.

The next few weeks of my pregnancy were just that way—heavy with the fog that settles cold and stagnant, when our fears rise wild before us. One day I thought I was getting better and the next day things seemed worse. It was hard to tell. Anemia was weakening me physically and the iron pills were barely towing their weight. All of it, fog.

I wanted to trust the ground in front of me, the Rock I was raised on, but muscle memory is slow when every step feels new. My reflexes wanted to lock the brakes. I get you, Moses, as I think the same—*What about me, God?* The truth of Ecclesiastes 3:14 echoed quietly in my subconscious:

> I know that whatever God does, it shall be forever. Nothing can be added to it, and nothing taken from it. God does it that men should fear before Him. (Ecclesiastes 3:14)

This is where the truth we learn in the daylight helps us find our footing in the thickest fog. There is a refining that occurs in these pure and painful places, and only what is true remains.

We can choose to give way to the fear that is in front of us, that real fear hedging nearer, stirring bitter tears, and stealing our peace. We can crouch low and scramble to sweep up the shards of glass with our bare hands. Or we can lean into the immutability of God, His unchanging nature for all of eternity.

He is unchanging that we should fear Him—the God before us, inside of us, hemming us in all around, incomprehensibly bigger than the fear in front of us. We have a critical choice in our fear here.

These words formed slowly in days and appointments. Maybe like Moses, I had no light-bulb moment. I wasn't Paul, blinded roadside when clarity came something fierce. Clarity, faith, came in more slowly, as I chose to trust the One who goes before rather than what I saw in front of me.

You are God, I prayed. *Unchanging. The only One worthy of my fear. My limited nature and what I see in front of me does not matter, God, because this is who you are.*

Something incredible happens when we shift our gaze. Like Peter on the water when we turn our darting and frantic eyes from the crashing waves to the Holy One, not removing our fear, but rather reorienting it, our feet land firm again. No more sinking. Held.

Do you see how that works? We aren't fearless here, we *fear Him* here. The world may call it fearless, but we move anew in the light of the One deserving our fear. David captured it beautifully in Psalm 29. Read this with me slowly, friend. It's who He is.

Give unto the LORD, O you mighty ones,
Give unto the LORD glory and strength.

Give unto the LORD the glory due to His name;
Worship the LORD in the beauty of holiness.

The voice of the LORD is over the waters;
The God of glory thunders;
The LORD is over many waters.

The voice of the LORD is powerful;
The voice of the LORD is full of majesty.

The voice of the LORD breaks the cedars,
Yes, the LORD splinters the cedars of Lebanon.

He makes them also skip like a calf,
Lebanon and Sirion like a young wild ox.

The voice of the LORD divides the flames of fire.

The voice of the LORD shakes the wilderness;
The LORD shakes the Wilderness of Kadesh.

The voice of the LORD makes the deer give birth,
And strips the forests bare;
And in His temple everyone says, "Glory!"

The LORD sat enthroned at the Flood,
And the LORD sits as King forever.

The LORD will give strength to His people;
The LORD will bless His people with peace.

This is a God of action. The unchanging One who sees and thunders, powerful and majestic. The One whose voice breaks and splinters and divides. The One who shakes and strips and gives. He sits enthroned, granting strength, blessing, peace.

Are you beginning to catch a glimpse of who He is? Find Him here, in your fear. It changes everything. We will never understand our fear rightly until we view it in light of a limitless and unchanging God.

Thank God the story doesn't end with Moses at the burning bush, or me wrapped tight in fear now months into a difficult pregnancy, or you in whatever circumstance you find yourself right now. It doesn't have to end when the sharp words fly, when the bad news lands, or when the upheaval feels like it might split you in two. We know better than to deny the fear, but God is so gracious with our learning, patient with our clumsy attempts to begin to live this out. Our hope for fleeing the sin that plagues us is a greater view of the God who has freed us. So we start here, lifting our gaze smack in the middle of all that is hard and scary, fearing Him, knowing and understanding Him. And then we keep pressing in. We might not know exactly *what* to do, but remember Solomon told us where to start:

> The fear of the LORD is the beginning of wisdom, and the knowledge of the Holy One is understanding. (Proverbs 9:10)

We must know who He is to understand how He works and what He does. And wisdom has always, *will always*, begin with fearing Him.

CHAPTER 6

Smaller Gods

Not knowing how to feed the spirit, we try to muffle its demands in distractions. Instead of stilling the center, the axis of the wheel, we add more centrifugal activities to our lives—which tend to throw us off balance.

Anne Morrow Lindbergh, The Gift from the Sea

Weeks turned into months and my story was much the same. Chronic, intermittent bleeding. Strong heartbeat. Steady growth. It's strange how quickly *abnormal* can become your normal.

The twenty-week ultrasound was fast approaching and we were thrilled to find out the gender of our baby. We'd had our fill of surprises. We weren't interested in playing any wait-and-see games.

It had been almost a month since we peeked in on this life growing inside me. Steady unsteadiness meant fewer doctors' appointments in recent weeks. We approached this date with almost normal excitement. Today we would see our baby. We would attach appropriate pronouns to this little life. Today we would share exciting news with people we loved.

I settled myself onto the familiar ultrasound table and made small talk with the tech while she prepped her surroundings in a practiced manner. Warm jelly on the belly, adjust the screen for patient viewing, grab the ultrasound wand, and go to work.

I focused hard on the screen. My ultrasound skills were increasing. What had looked puzzling and almost alien with my firstborn was beginning to make sense to me now. Dozens of ultrasounds had sharpened my skills and I quietly wondered if I would be able to determine the sex of the baby before the ultrasound tech declared it. I liked the idea of this unspoken competition I had going on.

But when her wand connected with my belly, nothing made sense. My newfound skills evaporated and I felt as though I was looking at an ultrasound for the first time again. Like groping for a familiar anchor when the lights go out, my eyes scanned the screen, hoping to make sense of something, anything. A steady heartbeat pulsed through the speaker, but nothing looked right.

Confused, I conceded and looked instead at the ultrasound tech. Her poker face was solid but her vague words were everything. "Excuse me for just a minute," she lobbed softly. "I need to go get a doctor."

I knew nothing at all and yet more than enough in that moment. Hot tears surged to the surface without warning and Ross reached for my hand. Together we waited to learn more about whatever hard and real and scary things lay ahead.

Last year I sat at a retreat and listened to a beautifully vulnerable woman share the story of losing her daughter only months earlier. Barely a year old, her healthy little girl caught an uncommon fever and became septic. After days of anguish, praying their most fervent prayers beside their daughter's tiny hospital bed, this mama grabbed her husband's hands and hit the floor right there in the hospital room. They offered up their purest confession: "Forgive us, O God, for holding on to anything more tightly than we are holding on to you."

My breathing stilled as I received her words. *Who does that?* I thought. I write about courage and faith. I talk about courage and faith. But this posture in real pain shocked me. How is that kind of boldness, that kind of humility, that kind of *brave* even possible? But I know the answers to my own questions. Abraham did.[1] Hagar did.[2] Jochebed, Moses' mother, did.[3] Hannah did.[4] Mary did.[5] This brave, bereaved mother did. Each and every one of these faithful parents, caught in gut-wrenching pain, locked eyes with God and were empowered by the Spirit to obedience. They feared God more than what was in front of them. They trusted God, obeyed God, and loved God more than the tiny people we as mothers have this natural tendency to strangle and suffocate with our affection.

Each of the above stories involved parents with an acute awareness of who God is and who we are in light of Him. These were listeners who had thriving prayer lives and were paying close attention when God spoke. They were average people committed to fierce obedience who were willing to walk that obedience out in ways that were grittier and more painful than most of us can imagine. They were not willing to put their calling as parents before their calling as children of God. That's a trade that is increasingly glorified in our culture, but it's vital to recognize that our children, our spouses, our career, our health and fitness, etc., while wonderful gifts, they make pretty terrible gods.

I can feel the lump in my throat just putting those words on a page, friend, because we're inching into protective territory here. These are things we love and value, things we prioritize, sacrifice for, and pour our lives into. They matter. But there must be boundaries—the righteousness of these relationships is dependent upon their right place in our lives. They were never intended to be our first love. *What do we fear more than God?* Our pain-points often answer that question for us.

Where do you get easily offended and hurt? What frustrates you and makes you angry? What rattles you and shakes your sense of what is right in the world? What do you cling tightly to? What do you fear most? Listen closely to your own answers; they speak loudly to what your heart values most.

Jen Wilkin cuts to the quick with her breakdown of idolatry in her book *None Like Him*: "We confuse stewardship with ownership, viewing ourselves as givers of life. We take the gifts God has given us to steward—gifts like leadership, administration, and mercy—and we use them to fuel our 'creator complex,' employing them to build our own kingdoms instead of his."[6]

The lump in my throat just grew bigger. Soon it will be threatening my oxygen supply. How many good gifts, which *He* has given, have I owned like a greedy toddler? I've shouted, "Mine!" in a hundred more sophisticated ways and thrown a full-on fit undetected by the outside world, but undeniable to the One who sees me.

Why me, God? I wonder. When there are teens having babies who can't even care for them, women who don't even want them, why me? Why me, God, when the plan feels like a flop, when the event turns out all wrong, when I've been trying hard with my marriage and *he* clearly hasn't? Why me, God, when I've been faithful and I've prayed brave, when I adjusted the inputs and did all of the right things? Have you been here, friend, carefully checking all of the boxes, following the recipe and felt flat frustrated, disappointed, angry, when the result is not what you intended, not what you want?

The creator complex Wilkin speaks of becomes glaring. Our bitter questions fly in the face of the gospel we profess to believe—saved by His grace alone, not because of anything we've done.[7] We so easily, almost naturally, use the gifts He has given and build a kingdom of expectation, a kingdom we believe should produce results in ways that we see fit. *Oh God, forgive us.*

The subtle shift in this line of thinking is everything. Our gaze strays from the One worthy to everything else we can squeeze, control, and slowly idolize. *My* time, *my* kids, *my* friendships, *my* marriage, material things all begin to fill a void. They become a means to an end, things we are trusting more than God. They become smaller gods that we focus on and worship.

When We Try to Replace God

I hope you can feel how easy and almost natural this is to turn our sights to smaller gods. Our affection for sin always is. This is nothing new. Look at the mess with Abram, Sarai, and Hagar in Genesis 16—a husband and wife who longed to conceive and a maid who was about to go beyond the call of duty. God's promised heir was too slow coming, and the quick fix of a surrogate seemed to be a simple helping along of God's good plan with man's good ideas. Tell me you have never had a few good ideas, a few brilliant suggestions, to help along God's good plan, friend. Abram and Sarai's story is a little strange in our culture, but the heart behind it? *We get that.* And the fallout is always heartbreaking:

- Her mistress became despised in her eyes (v. 4).
- "My wrong be upon you! . . . I became despised in her eyes" (v. 5).
- "Do to her as you please" (v. 6).
- She fled from her presence (v. 6).

A faithful maid becomes a second-choice wife. The bitterness of being used spills over and becomes cancerous. A strong leader of a husband gets weak-kneed in the midst of this hormonal hatred and abdicates his authority. Brokenness is the only by-product of our "good idea." Brokenness that outlives these people. Brokenness that an almighty God can (and will) most certainly redeem, but the pain and hurt it causes is real and deep.

This is what it looks like when we replace Him—subtle shifts, our perceived wisdom replacing His perfect will. Our sin tendency, our creator complex writes the worst soap operas. Real ones, unscripted ones, with brokenness and fallout that trickles down for generations. And in moments of heartache, on an ultrasound bed receiving devastating news, a loved one who continues to choose destruction, or the long and echoing waiting room of life, we tend to usurp the authority of the God we profess to believe and turn to our own wisdom instead.

Marshall Segal, in a beautiful piece written for *Desiring God*, explains it this way:

> Spiritually, we struggle to make sense of our surroundings. The eyes of our heart squint, searching for even a fragment of the light of Christ. In those days (or weeks, or years), we will be tempted to try and dispel the darkness—to alleviate the discomfort of waiting on God—by lighting our life a thousand other ways. Instead of navigating the deeper darkness by patiently following the voice of God, we will look for a torch of

our own making. Isaiah warned a despondent and wandering Israel against walking by theirs: "Behold, all you who kindle a fire, who equip yourselves with burning torches! Walk by the light of your fire, and by the torches that you have kindled! This you have from my hand: you shall lie down in torment" (Isaiah 50:11). God's warning is clear: if we walk by the light of our own torches when darkness falls, we will eventually be burned by them.[8]

Do you see the very burning that Segal describes here in the story of Abraham, Sarah, and Hagar? God had a beautiful and promised plan, but every one of them was burned by the light of their own torch. Thank God none of that is beyond redemption, but our idolization of our own good ideas is most certainly not without hurt and pain and scars. Look side to side in the lives of those around you. Look back in your own history, in your family, and in the lives of those you love. I bet you can quite easily see the same thing. Many hands and hearts singed by the light of our torches.

On one hand we say we know God, we reach and grasp for Him, become rooted and try to comprehend the width and length and depth and height of His love. We nod with the preacher on Sunday morning who reads Isaiah 46:9: "Remember the former things of old, for I am God and there is no other; I am God and there is none like me."

Yes, God, this is who you are. We sing right along with Hillsong about the God who speaks galaxies into motion and get teary at Carl Boberg's famous lines, "Oh Lord my God, when I in awesome wonder, consider all the worlds thy hands hath made."[9] But we meet a bump in the road and our reflex becomes *us.*

Our readiness and ability to fear Him in the big and hard things will always be a direct result of fearing Him in the small and daily ones. How we respond when it feels as though a rug has been snatched from beneath us, when our mind spins blank and we don't know what just happened, becomes a reflex of the heart work done beforehand. God is exceedingly gracious to walk and grow with us. Go back and read through Moses' calling at the burning bush *again* and watch that slow and gentle growth and guidance play out firsthand. God walks him patiently into a big and scary calling, but it is essential that Moses keeps his eyes on God, leaning not on his own understanding every step of the way. That's how it's done, friend. In the desert, on an ultrasound table, and wherever you find yourself right now.

Fear is a given. What we fear is what we see as worthy and in desperation, our souls get hungry for news, for hope, for something steady to hold on to. And in choosing something else, in our idolatry of anything that will soothe or console, our quick fix, we are doubting God.

What have we traded for God? To what or to whom have we given His rightful place? May this serve as a clear reminder: He alone is worthy of honor and glory. He alone is worthy of our fear.

> Who among you fears the LORD and obeys the voice of his servant? Let him who walks in darkness and has no light trust in the name of the LORD and rely on his God. (Isaiah 50:10 ESV)

> This is eternal life, that they may know you, the only true God, and Jesus Christ whom You have sent. (John 17:3)

May we fear, obey, rely on, and know Him alone.

CHAPTER 7

On Trend

I like to read new translations of the Bible and Prayer Book for new insights, for shocks of discovery and humor, but I don't want to discard the old, as though it were transitory as last year's fashions.

Madeleine L'Engle, Walking on Water:
Reflections on Faith & Art

Moments like these are surreal. Dreamy in the worst way. We grope for answers, facts, statistics, and yet nothing sticks, nothing soothes. Our brains go echo-y, our hearts numb to everything except the hurt. My doctor spoke softly, delivering her words to my exposed wound with careful honesty. It all sounded flat in my head, and all I could think was no. *No, no, no*—as if toddler-style defiance might be more effective as an adult. Turns out, it isn't.

You have lost all of your amniotic fluid.

Without amniotic fluid, your baby's lungs will be unable to develop.

I'm sorry.

Our best guess is that you will deliver full term, but your baby will be unable to breathe, unable to live.

I'm so sorry.

That's all I remember. That, and the *no* throbbing inside me. No, to the doctor delivering these words. No, to God for bringing me this far only to land here. No, to a baby who can't breathe; twenty more weeks of a pregnancy that will not produce life. I couldn't bear to look Ross in the eye. I heard the doctor spout a few statistics, say words like *sub-chronic bleeding*, but I just wanted her to stop. I had reached capacity. I couldn't take anything more in.

But her next words came out slower, quieter. Maybe it was just me, my hearing and understanding folding in on each other, tunneling in on me, shutting out the world. They sounded like a limp, serpentine olive branch.

You have the option to terminate the pregnancy.

I finally met Ross's gaze and neither of us even flinched. The *no* that had been pulsing inside of me, trembling both weak and strong, came out clear from both of us.

No. That is not an option. The words tasted of both relief and fear at the very same time.

The belief we procure, the truth we understand, the faith we form in fair weather becomes foundational in the storm, friend. When words won't come and your mind goes numb, the truth planted long before that moment, in slower seasons, rises to the surface, becomes reflexive. And those quiet days we spent reading the Word, slowly knowing God, taking the tiniest steps toward wisdom, matter more than we ever realized. But there is an alarming trend to make truth a little more palatable, up to date with the times, we might say. Have you seen it? Truth spun so thin it begins to get a little crooked? When the church, in an effort to engage culture, begins to look more and more like the world? These shades of gray, these subtle shifts matter, friend, and they will steal our courage, leaving us afraid.

Knowing I AM

I can be a trendy God-girl. Maybe that happens when you've been in the church for a long time? I had a Precious Moments Bible in the '80s. In the '90s I wore those WWJD (What Would Jesus Do) rubber-band bracelets, and at the turn of the century, I started using language like "God thing" and "Jesus people" and "bless." Don't tell me Christianity doesn't have trends of its own.

On a larger scale, our tone and rhetoric has changed as well. Long past the hell, fire, and brimstone sermons of the past, cyclical in generations long gone, we've fallen into the age of grace, where the preeminent attribute of God that gets distributed, reported, liked, and shared is His love for us. This is real and vital, to be certain, but our trends are worth paying attention to.

Why do we zero in on certain attributes of God at the neglect of others? Our sin tendency causes us to follow patterns of the world, to make our faith palatable or relatable or cool. We follow statistics closely. We predict trends that will penetrate hearts, and while there is value in meeting people where they are, part of the profound beauty of our God is that He is unchanging. The gospel is unchanging.

In theological terms we call this His immutability, and it's a big deal. This means who He *was* at Creation is who He *is* today.

For I am the LORD, I do not change. (Malachi 3:6)

Jesus Christ is the same yesterday, today, and forever. (Hebrews 13:8)

This truth means what we learn about His character in Scripture—His faithfulness and mercy, His wrath and justice—is tangible truth we can be certain of today. For a woman trying to process the wild tide of emotions that I felt in that doctor's office or wherever you find yourself right now—dealing with weighty trials or the road bumps and unexpected challenges of everyday life—the steady anchor of an unchanging God is *huge.*

But as believers, we tend to let our pendulum swing wide over decades and generations, we prioritize the attributes of God like trending topics as if we are unable to hold the balance of who He is. The tension that He is both grace *and* truth. He is mercy *and* wrath. He is justice *and* fear *and* love.

In some ways I get it. Most of us have very little healthy representation of this in our own lives so we cling to what we know, what we can understand in the present. But our limited understanding does not, cannot, change who He is.

God, who has ruled forever, will hear me and humble them. For my enemies refuse to change their ways; they do not fear God. (Psalm 55:19 NLT)

When God met Moses at that burning bush, He gave himself a name. I AM. I promise it's not because He had no other words to offer. Have you seen the complexity and wild creativity of the world God created? Have you stared at a praying mantis lately or watched the mating dance of the birds-of-paradise? Google that, friend. Have you stared at the delicate layers of a camellia or studied the stars He spoke into existence? It was not from a lack of creativity or vocabulary that this God of ours gave us His name. He is creative beyond our wildest imaginings. It is because those are the only words that can hold the complexity, the capacity, of who He is. I AM THAT I AM.

Pause here. Try to let your mind absorb that for half a minute and then tell me why we try to get cute and trendy. He doesn't need us to make Him palatable. He doesn't need us to lessen the tension in the mystery, to play an angle or attribute. In fact, it's pretty embarrassing that we are prone to doing this. We sift through Scripture for the "good" ones that fit our current need. We read the chapters that play well to our emotional state, and it feels like a good idea until we begin to weigh that at face value.

Think about that for a hot minute and it looks something like crafting God in our own fashion. It's hauntingly similar to what the Israelites did out in the desert—begging for their jewelry to be turned into a golden calf—fashioning a god that looked a little more palatable, presentable, popular, and in proximity. A God they wouldn't have to wait for, when that waiting was for their good. It was all for their good. Can you see it, friend? He molds us, right where we are, through trial and monotony and pain and fear. He can be trusted because we know who He is. We don't need to mold and shape *Him*.

Do We Even Know Him?

I've long been fascinated with the story of Jesus feeding the five thousand. Right after Jesus' birth, death, and resurrection . . . and maybe creation, this is one of the first Bible stories we learn as children, isn't it?

It has all the elements that resonate with kids—a miracle with a child involved, some very tangible and easy-to-understand resources—fishes and loaves—multiplied until men were collecting the overflow in baskets. The story is easy to love.

But this is another one of those passages (get used to it, I feel this way about the entire canon of Scripture) that is pretty amazing to meet with the maturity of adulthood.

Read with me slowly here and let's see what we find when we dissect this passage in layers, beginning in Mark 6:30–31:

> The apostles gathered to Jesus and told Him all things, both what they had done and what they had taught. And He said to them, "Come aside by yourself to a deserted place and rest for a while." For there were many coming and going and they did not even have time to eat.

Please tell me you get this. These guys have been *busy*. So busy they didn't even have time to eat a decent meal. Feel free to nod, mama. Yes, you grabbing a handful of goldfish crackers or pilfering remains off your kid's lunch plate as you toss it in the dishwasher and start another load. Or you, friend, subbing lunch for the protein bar from the bottom of your purse, working right through the lunch hour, chained to your office desk by a stiff deadline. We know what don't-even-have-time-to-eat weary feels like, right? *That's* where the disciples were as Mark unpacks this familiar story.

> They departed to a deserted place in the boat by themselves. But the multitudes saw them departing, and many knew Him and ran there on foot from all the cities. They arrived before them and came together to Him. (vv. 32–33)

Ah, shoot! In lesser terms, you know this too. I mean, obviously you are not the miracle-working Messiah being chased down. But you know what it's like to finally finish the dishes and turn around to see a few more left on the stove, right? You know what it's like to be done, *done* parenting for the night and have one more kid who wants a drink and wants to talk. You know what it's like to have an overwhelming schedule for the day and then the kindest, most generous person you know, the one who would help you out in a heartbeat, asks you for help. *Ughhh.* Jesus and the disciples are here, minus the grumbling and complaining part.

The very next verse (v. 34) tells us of Jesus' response:

> Jesus, when He came out, saw a great multitude and was moved with compassion for them, because they were like sheep not having a shepherd. So He began to teach them many things.

So Jesus and the disciples spent the rest of their day pouring out to this crowd of people, and eventually the disciples started checking their watches. I'm thinking they knew they'd done a good deed, but they had about reached their limit and it was mealtime. Remember, they were already skipping meals when they started this day, right? So they decided to share their insight with Jesus:

> Send them away, that they may go into the surrounding country and villages and buy themselves bread; for they have nothing to eat. (v. 36)

And Jesus shocked them with His plain response: "You give them something to eat" (v. 37).

Uh, yeah. That's pretty clear, right? With one sentence, one command, He was asking about so much more. *Don't you see who I am? Do you not know me yet? Don't you see the power that is available to you?* They thought they knew Him, and it turned out they didn't know Him at all.

This is what concerns me, friend. This is where we find ourselves in comfortable Christianity. Many of us were raised in church with, at the very least, the idea of it being a good moral compass, but we have pared down and picked out the "good" Scriptures so long, we have watered down and made the gospel more "loving," more seeker friendly, to the complete neglect of the rest of it. And I wonder, do we even know who He is anymore?

If, as A.W. Tozer succinctly stated, "What comes into our minds when we think of God is the most important thing about us,"[1] is true, then this question deserves an answer. But for now let's follow those disciples in Mark 6 and see how they fared.

The miracle most of us know from memory took place. Five loaves, two fish. Jesus blessed it, broke it, and proceeded to fully feed five thousand men plus all of the women and children who were with them. The leftovers filled twelve baskets.

This was a big deal. Don't let those facts slide by you in familiarity. This wasn't just provision, which most certainly would have been enough in my opinion, and I'm guessing those hungry people would have agreed with me. Two fish and five loaves pieced into appetizers for thousands, a little something to hold them over, keep them comfortable, until they could get to the next village, would have still been miraculous. But minimalist hospitality wasn't what Jesus would do here. The NLT says, "They all ate as much as they wanted and afterward, the disciples picked up twelve baskets of leftover bread and fish" (Mark 6:42–43).

That's wild! This is the God Paul wrote about when he told the church at Ephesus, "Now to Him who is able to do exceedingly abundantly above all that we ask or think . . ." (Ephesians 3:20). This is Him at work. The exceedingly abundantly above, God. *Do we know Him?*

Directly after this miracle, the very next verse in Mark 6 says, "Immediately He made His disciples get into the boat and go before Him to the other side, to Bethsaida, while He sent the multitude away. And when He had sent them away, He departed to the mountain to pray" (v. 45).

The order of events here is important. God was taking care of the masses and teaching His disciples who He was at the very same time.

On the boat to Bethsaida, another familiar story took place. Stick with me here, we're traveling some distance, but I promise we will see this all sync together soon.

A storm picked up on the sea, and Jesus was watching from the shore, His disciples straining to row in it. Early in the morning, Jesus walked out on the water to meet His disciples, who had now been fighting this storm for hours. When they saw Him, the very Jesus they spent the entire previous day with, they thought He was a ghost. They didn't even recognize who He was, and they were terrified. But He commanded their calm, stepped into the boat, into their crisis, and the storm ceased. And Mark tells us that "they were greatly amazed in themselves beyond measure, and marveled" (v. 51).

And this next verse is everything, friend: "For they had not understood about the loaves, because their heart was hardened" (v. 52).

Ugh. Do you see the link? These disciples were standing on the calm boat, greatly amazed—some translations say completely astounded—and surprised, because in all of their time with Jesus thus far, their hearts were still too hard to take it all in. The root word for *hard* here means calloused, dull, or to lose the power of understanding. They had time in the game, first-person accounts of His power, and they still couldn't see it.

This is my concern with pop-culture Christianity, friend. This is my concern with trends and cycles and picking and choosing our attributes of God. Of zooming in on the command to *not fear* at the disregard and complete neglect of the command *to fear*. Of crafting a foundation of fearlessness, of courage that we think exists somewhere deep inside ourselves. We do this at the risk of *what*? At the denial and exclusion of *what?* Do we even know Him? Are we in the boat, blind and scared, missing the reality of His power displayed right in front of us?

Trendy or not, we cannot afford to miss Him here. Caught up in mainstream Christianity, we are not to fashion God to our ways and means, our time and place—narrowing our gaze to only part of who He is while neglecting the rest. I want more, not less, of the truth of who He is. I want more, not less, knowledge of Him. The fear of the Lord is the beginning of wisdom. Let's not scan over that, run past it, declare it out of style. This is who He is. This is His gift of provision for us.

Let's step right into it, friend. Fully. Let's hunger and thirst to know *all* of who He is. This is pressing in. *This* is choosing brave. Not another buzz word, not more of us. It's stepping closer to that burning bush, not because of who we are, but because of who He was and is. I AM. The story He writes, is still writing, is beautiful.

CHAPTER 8

Curiosity and Obedience

The most crushing lie a life can hold on to is that life is supposed to avoid suffering, avoid loss, avoid anything that breaks.

Ann Voskamp, *The Broken Way:*
A Daring Path into the Abundant Life

When the day comes that tragedy rocks your world, when the diagnosis or the voice on the other end of the phone unleashes an earthquake that sucks the air straight from your lungs, something equally unexpected happens at the very same time. The rest of the world keeps right on going. It just does. Mail carriers deliver mail and line cooks flip burgers. Traffic lights run their sequence, bills still need to be paid, and grass grows. It's bizarre, and yet normal.

My understanding of this phenomena came rather quickly as red and blue lights spiraled in the rearview mirror on our drive home from that doctor's appointment. Ross is prone to driving faster than the recommended speed limit, possibly even more so on the day of a bitter diagnosis. We both knew those swirling lights were for our benefit.

There are times in life when you may rhetorically ask yourself if this day could get any worse. And there are times when the answer is yes, very much *yes*.

As the officer approached our car, I willed my numb brain and body to work. *Insurance. Registration. Katie, you can do this.* While Ross rolled down the window and greeted the officer, I unlatched the glove compartment, which responded like a tightly wound jack-in-the-box, flying open and spilling its contents at my feet. Even worse was that its contents consisted almost entirely of my secret stash of overnight-capacity, thick-as-a-bed-mattress, maxi pads. What appeared to be a year's supply tumbled out like confetti and landed in a pile at my feet.

Surviving these months with bleeding that came in gushing fits and starts, I had learned to be prepared. While some women grab breath mints or maybe their lipstick as they rush out the door, I got in the habit of grabbing an extra maxi pad and stashing it in the glove box, just in case I found myself in a situation where I needed it. This was not that particular situation, but friend, I was prepared.

I didn't even look up to meet the shocked stares of my husband and the police officer as I grabbed wildly for those pastel-colored packages and started stuffing them into my purse. Maybe hiding the evidence could hide the awkward too? The tears and snot that had been slow and steady since we left the doctor's office started to reach a new level of intensity when mixed with frustration and a healthy dose of embarrassment. Looking back, I probably should have busted one of those little packages open and just stuck it to my face at that point, but I was still grasping at any last hope of decorum.

"Ma'am, are you okay?" It was interesting how quickly this officer would choose to forego his normal line of questioning. Clearly, this was not his normal traffic stop. Maybe he should have stuck to his usual questions because the answer to this was pretty obvious. My words weren't coming out. What do you even say? Ross interceded, trying to help. "She's fine. We just came from a—"

"No, sir!" the officer interjected abruptly. "You need to let the woman speak for herself."

I didn't pick up on the officer's suspicion of domestic disturbance as quickly as my husband did, but with both of them now waiting on the weeping woman to respond, I managed to alleviate the officer's suspicion, and he cleared us to get back on the road with both a warning and condolences. Even while tragedy was a cliff in front of us, the world was definitely still spinning.

Whether we inadvertently choose our challenges or they choose us, we almost always have some level of ability to choose our response. Think about it for a minute. Think about the tough times you chose, directly or indirectly. You chose to diet. You chose to cut corners on your taxes. You chose to neglect going to see your doctor. Each of these decisions can present real and serious challenges for you down the road—now you get to choose how to respond. Will you become frustrated and shut down? Will you be full of shame or guilt and stonewall the world around you? Or will you lift your eyes, open your hands, even in hard and hurting moments, and step toward what God might have for you *here*?

Conversely, your sister's marriage may fall apart, your parents may manage their finances unwisely, or you may have a high-risk pregnancy. Each of these things, while you did not choose them, may present real and serious challenges for you— now you get to choose how to respond.

Of all the appropriate biblical responses we might think up in these situations—we could pray and fast and quote Scripture and seek wise counsel—I want you to consider something a little less obvious but of vital importance—*curiosity*.

Do we even think of that as a biblical response? Maybe not, but I would argue *we should*.

Curiosity is an attribute we frequently see in children—the young who are still enamored with, and learning so much about, the world around them. But when we begin to understand the immensity of our Creator, the knowledge of whom our minds have not even brushed the surface of—should we be any different?

Becoming Curious

Let's look at Scripture and see how some of the notables dealt with life's challenges. We already met Moses at the burning bush. Remember his very normal response when he first saw that bush: "I will now turn aside and see this great sight, why the bush does not burn."

Describe Moses' response in one word. Was he brave or bold? Was he deliberate or hesitant? Possibly any of those, but Scripture doesn't say that. All we know is that he was curious. He saw something unique going on, for better or worse, and he was simply curious. The next sentence is telling: "When the LORD saw that he turned aside to look, God called to him from the midst of the bush and said, 'Moses, Moses!' And he said, 'Here I am'" (Exodus 3:4).

When did God call to Moses?

After he turned aside to look.

Isn't that fascinating? Moses caught sight of something unique. His curiosity caused him to lean in, to move *toward* it, and at *that* moment, God spoke.

This isn't an isolated incident. We looked at Joshua 5 earlier, but let's mine the depths a little more. Fresh off crossing the Jordan River, Joshua was moving toward Jericho when he looked up and saw, standing before him, a man with His sword drawn. I would call that a challenge demanding a response, wouldn't you? The very next verse gives us the play by play on Joshua's choice: "Joshua went to Him and said to Him, 'Are You for us or for our adversaries?'" (v. 13).

Can you even imagine? This is not intuitive. This is not a natural response—moving *toward* a particularly serious situation. If it were me, I would be carefully backing away, putting a little distance between me and the guy standing on guard. At best I would freeze, stand still. But that's not what Joshua does here. He moves forward with a question. This is holy courage mixed with curiosity. He needs to know. "Are you for us or for our adversaries?" As leader of the troops behind him, he had a job and Joshua leaned in and got it done.

I have to think that the response Joshua received surprised him just a bit: "No, but as Commander of the army of the LORD I have now come" (v. 14).

And Joshua fell on his face to the earth and worshiped. "What does my Lord say to His servant?" The change in Joshua's positioning is critical. He moved toward what caught his attention, *leaned in,* and then the Commander of the Lord's army spoke, revealing His identity along with a specific battle plan for the Israelites to conquer Jericho.

If we limit curiosity to children, we may very well miss out on some of the most important callings God has for us. When He calls us to become like children (see Matthew 18:3), it isn't a stretch to believe this is what He is saying—be humble, be teachable, be free from pride and positioning, be eager to learn, be curious. It was from this very place that Moses and Joshua leaned in and God responded.

I don't always think to start *here* when studying these familiar stories. I think of the Israelite exodus or those walls crumbling in Jericho, but this is critical for the invitations of our daily life. Can we be curious to the work God is doing? Are we interested in the things He places in front of us? Do we look at our challenges, whether we chose them or not, as opportunities to lean in and hear Him, to potentially know Him and fear Him? If not, why?

In retrospect it's often easier to see God moving in and amid our story. We can look back at difficult times and see how our faith grew or how His provision was evident, but as we learn to fear God, the facts of our past must become the fuel of our faith in the present and future. This is who God is. Read about Him and know Him. Watch how He is at work and know Him. And when we begin to know Him, we should naturally be more curious and attentive, hungry to see His hand at work in our every day. When we seek, we will find, and I'm confident that our curiosity when properly aligned with the truth of the gospel, honors Him.

Choosing Obedience

Neither Moses nor Joshua nor Mary nor even Paul stopped at simply being curious. Paul's words in Acts are some of my favorite. Meeting the Lord on his way to Damascus, Paul was trembling and astonished and asked questions: "Who are you, Lord?" and "What do you want me to do?" In an instant, Paul got it. He understood. *God, I want to know who you are. And what do I do with that knowledge?* Those questions are the exact result of curiosity and a heart ready to pursue obedience.

These are the questions—whether we met the Lord ten days or ten years ago—we must be asking.

Do you see how curiosity and obedience work together? As we learn what it means to fear the Lord, as we uncover Scripture that we have breezed by for years, we begin to see how much we have left on the table. We begin to see the importance of slowing down and wondering, of asking Paul-style questions about who God is and what He wants us to do.

"God," we can ask, "what do you mean when you say in Psalm 112, 'Blessed is the man who fears the LORD . . . he will not be afraid of evil . . . his heart is established: he will not be afraid'?"

Can we move toward these verses and be curious about the words He left for us, the words *He chose* for us? If His Word really is a lamp and a light, should we not pause, turn and look, and ask Him what this really means?

Could obedience possibly look a whole lot less like our ten-step process to overcoming fear, our tired antidotes, Band-Aids, even Scripture we apply hastily, out of context, or at the neglect of what the rest of Scripture is saying? Could it possibly look more like paying attention to where He is moving, moving toward Him with holy courage, and choosing to follow wherever He leads?

Just as with Paul and Joshua and Moses, He shows up in our every day, and paying attention is only part of our job. Obedience, moving in and amid what He is doing, where He is calling, and how He leads, is a gritty choice that is ours to make. Are we brave enough to say yes to that?

This is why I urge you to slow your pace, friend. Read closely. Listen hard as you learn and unpack what it means to know and fear God. Ask God to give you eyes and ears tuned afresh to His voice, so that by His Holy Spirit, He can teach you anything you have neglected to see in His living and active Word. Get curious and get moving. Because by evidence of who He is and what He has done, we know that when His people move nearer, He speaks. And when we obey, He is able to use us in ways we never would have imagined.

CHAPTER 9

Vulnerability

We fear men so much, because we fear God so little.

G.K. Chesterton, Orthodoxy

There's an unseen guard that drops when you have a baby in your belly. Particularly when that belly becomes obviously pregnant. Conversations come from nowhere. "When are you due?" becomes the low hanging fruit of small talk; even strangers will grasp for that with ease. Women will candidly share labor and delivery stories that were never casual conversation before. The really brave ones will reach a hand to your belly like it's magnetic. Pregnancy is a bridge, a shared experience that seems to welcome input.

This fact becomes increasingly uncomfortable when your baby has an unavoidable, incurable death sentence in lieu of a delivery date, when the tiniest thought of your baby's life makes you weak in the knees, short of breath, and groping for something, anything, to steady yourself with. Surviving twenty weeks of *this* small talk felt like I was serving my own sentence. I wanted to avoid people and lock myself away for as long as it took.

But the UPS man showed up at my door. The florist delivered flowers. We went to church. I hated all of it—the talk, the hugs, the well-meaning words. I hated the vulnerability of it all.

My journal from those days captured my feelings honestly:

> It hurts. It hurts to be alone. It hurts to think, to know that so much more of this challenge lies ahead than behind me. I'm scared. I'm scared to go into labor. I'm scared that the baby will live past delivery but die in my arms. I'm scared to see the baby. I want to have faith, but I don't know how exactly, to open my heart to the possibility of a miracle. It feels so selfish not to do that for my baby, but I don't know how much more pain I can handle.

I have never felt more vulnerable than in the days after that diagnosis—vulnerable into my thoughts and emotions, and vulnerable to let others in the weakness of that space. Webster's dictionary says that vulnerability means capable of being physically or emotionally wounded.[1] That was it exactly. It already hurt, and the open exposure of raw wounds, not knowing how or when or *if* it would let up left me feeling completely untethered, at a loss, vulnerable.

Considering Webster's definition, it's surprising that vulnerability has actually become such a popular idea these days. You don't have to sit long among any group of women, inside or outside the church, to see the concept of vulnerability lauded and praised. Who knew being capable of being physically or emotionally wounded would be trendy? This trend might actually be helpful if we don't scarf down all the cultural fluff, all the self-focus, associated with it. Thankfully, Scripture doesn't leave us without direction here.

Arguably the most practical examples of vulnerability we see in Scripture come from David in the Psalms. The man after God's heart[2] opened his own heart far and wide to share his rugged thoughts and emotions in verse and song. And it wasn't always pretty.

> I am weary with my moaning; every night I flood my bed with tears; I drench my couch with my weeping. My eye wastes away because of grief; it grows weak because of all my foes. (Psalm 6:6–7 ESV)

> Be gracious to me, O LORD, for I am in distress; my eye is wasted from grief; my soul and my body also. For my life is spent with sorrow, and my years with sighing; my strength fails because of my iniquity, and my bones waste away. (Psalm 31:9–10 ESV)

> My heart is in anguish within me; the terrors of death have fallen upon me. Fear and trembling come upon me, and horror overwhelms me. And I say, "Oh, that I had wings like a dove! I would fly away and be at rest; yes, I would wander far away; I would lodge in the wilderness" (Psalm 55:4–7 ESV).

Besides being a more skillful writer, David's psalms don't read that differently from my own journal entry. He's hurt. Tears and grief are raging. He dreams of running away from it all. That is vulnerability, honesty that exposes weakness. But in that open exposure to wounding, that real risk of hurt, comes a most unique intimacy and knowing.

My friend Janessa gave birth to a son with Freeman Sheldon Syndrome, a disease that affects the joints, causing abnormalities in the head, hands, and feet. His legs are braced, he has a metal rod permanently implanted near his spine, and he walks with the help of a walker. His name is Edward, and with his sharp mind and easy candor, I am convinced he is the coolest nine-year-old you will ever meet, embracing his life, in the capacity he has been given, to a degree most of us only dream of. But in talking about her son recently, Janessa said living with his diagnosis has made her feel so vulnerable—vulnerable to the future, to what might happen next, not just for Edward, but for everyone. Her words resonated with me acutely, because that is what fear is, isn't it?

Fear is the face-to-face realization of our ineptness. It's the loss of control and the inability to manage outcomes. Fear is unexpected results, unintended consequences, the unknown.

Fear is the realization that we aren't God. We are not sovereign, without limits or unchanging. We are destructible, mortal, capable of being broken and hurt. Fear is the understanding that the pain is real. The popular term *vulnerability* leads us here, right? The realization of this potential wounding actually positions us to get to this hard truth. But as believers, this is where we get to take a hard right.

When we choose to fear God, that fear, which by biblical analysis means the very same thing as the fear of all that is vulnerable and real, scary, in front of us—when we reorient our fear, lifting our eyes from the *real* diagnosis, the *real* addicted husband, the *real* broken relationship toward the only One ever worthy of our fear—everything changes.

We give him our vulnerability and He gives us His strength. We turn that fear to Him and He says that His mercy rests on those who fear Him. Our God is the best return on vulnerability that we could ever imagine, because He operates in love toward those who fear Him, peace for those who fear Him, hope and a heritage, a banner for all those who fear His name.

Does it mean that bad diagnoses will not arrive? Absolutely not. When we look at the whole of Scripture, we will learn that really quick. But Paul reminds us that "the sufferings of this present time are not worthy to be compared with the glory which shall be revealed in us" (Romans 8:18). These are facts no other fear affords.

Do you see the trade-off we're making, the grace we are missing, when we allow the fear of the Lord to become a dusty, forsaken, watered-down, or dried-out concept? We are left to fight legitimate fear only with Band-Aids, some cheery self-talk, or a fake smile. He gave us more than that. He gave us himself. Why are we okay ignoring that?

In Psalm 31, which we just read above like an entry from David's journal, just after he tells us his eyes and bones are wasting away in grief, he stakes his claim, lifting his eyes from the "fear on every side," and he says, "Oh, how abundant is your goodness, which you have stored up for those who fear you and worked for those who take refuge in you, in the sight of the children of mankind!" (Psalm 31:19 ESV).

David has seen it, knows it, and proclaims it. The fear in front of him is real. The pain and grief are real. He is not fearless, but he chooses to fear God rather than the real and awful things in front of him. This is how it's done. This is choosing brave.

More poignantly we see Jesus Christ do the same in the garden of Gethsemane: "My soul is exceedingly sorrowful even to death. Stay here and watch with me," Matthew records in his Gospel.[3] Luke wrote, "Being in agony, He prayed more earnestly. Then His sweat became like great drops of blood falling down to the ground."[4] We're glimpsing the depths of His vulnerability here. His soul was laid bare before the Father. Being fully man, He grasped the pain He was in and both the pain and separation that lay directly ahead of Him. But amid that, we get the perfect example of what it means to lift our eyes: "Father, if it is Your will, take this cup away from Me; nevertheless, not My will, but Yours, be done" (Luke 22:42).

Fully consumed by real pain, Jesus lifted His eyes to the Father, because He knew who His Father was.

Hands and Hearts Wide Open

In her book *Suffering Is Never for Nothing*, Elisabeth Elliot, wife of the late missionary Jim Elliot, talks plainly about the realization of our struggles:

> Five days later I knew that Jim was dead. And that God's presence with me was not Jim's presence. That was a terrible fact. God's presence did not change the terrible fact that I was a widow and I expected to be a widow until I died. . . . God's presence did not change the fact of my widowhood. Jim's absence thrust me, forced me, hurried me to God, my hope and my only refuge. And I learned in that experience who God is. Who He is in a way that I could never have known otherwise. And so I can say to you that suffering is an irreplaceable medium through which I learned an indispensable truth. I am. I am the Lord. In other words, that God is God.[5]

This is the craziness of vulnerability, of hurt, of suffering, of fear. This is how some cancer patients stand at the end of a horrible battle and say, "If I had it to do all over again, I would." This is how we survive hard things without bitterness. It is hands-wide-open vulnerability before the Lord, a heart that chooses to fear Him rather than the real and scary standing in front of us.

My very next journal entry took on a different tone as I willed my eyes to look up:

> I am finding it easier to plan for my baby's death, write off all hope of life, even allow myself to prepare for the endurance of a funeral, rather than humble myself, fall on my face before God and ask Him to do a miracle. What am I thinking? I will proceed differently. I will have faith in my miraculous God. I will petition on behalf of my unborn child. If this is all I can

ever give to my baby, then that's okay, but I will not fail her now. She is a warrior in my womb, and I will be a warrior for her life.

I remember that moment vividly. I would be lying if I said I didn't believe then that my grit and gumption might change the prognosis. I'm sure a part of me thought I could out-faith the doctors or strong-arm God in prayer, just a little. My growing faith was not without weakness and the growth was never linear. But lifting my eyes, reorienting my fear was pivotal.

This is a corner you too have to turn, a choice you must make in the midst of the real and scary, friend. You can let the fear of what's in front of you consume you. You can let fear have jurisdiction over your heart, run rampant through your mind as you cast a hundred different scenarios and what-ifs. That's a real option. Or you can bow weak and vulnerable, you can lift your broken heart before the God who sees and knows and is willing to meet you right there in the thick of it. You can stand weak-kneed on the truth you learned in quiet moments, reorienting your fear toward the only One worthy. This is the very beginning of learning how to "count it all joy," as James 1:2 says, because we know the God who does marvelous things in truly unexpected places.

CHAPTER 10

Peace

In darkness God's truth shines most clear.

Corrie Ten Boom, The Hiding Place

Brooding clouds spat warm raindrops on my face as someone pushed the gurney from my house. Even the sky was gently sobbing. Apparently when you are en route to the ER, an umbrella is the least of everyone's concern. I didn't much mind. The dampness felt like life. Amid all that seemed broken, torn—not my real life and yet very much my reality—raindrops alighting my skin meant I was still feeling.

When suffering comes, our line of sight narrows, the walls close, and our breathing gets shallow. Everything looks and sounds different. It's hard to fathom how the world around us keeps spinning. So much of it doesn't matter. It's instant tunnel vision. Heavy and dark, you can't pull back the curtain. Because there isn't one. It's hard to let light in.

But something interesting happens here—our view becomes more focused. Cup your hands around your eyes and a hundred distractions disappear. You see less, but what you do see, you see more directly.

Labor came both sooner and faster than anyone expected—just days after that interrupted ultrasound when the doctor delivered the verdict. I was home and on the phone with my doctor as soon as the tightening in my abdomen became rhythmic, a pattern. This wasn't in any of the scenarios they had prepared me for. This wasn't in any of the scenarios I had prepared myself for. One searing rip through my belly and, in an instant, she was here. And there was only silence. The paramedics came and loaded me into the ambulance. I was trembling, overcome with fear. Of what exactly, I'm not even sure. Hope, in the form of my lifeless baby girl, had just been stripped from me, and the only thing I felt was fear. Because when pain reaches the pulpy parts of your heart, the grown-up version of a newborn's soft spot, when that last fragmented shard of hope you have held fast to shatters, dissolves, the world feels nothing but empty, hollow, and scary.

That's where I was in that ambulance. The steely doors clanged shut and the cold detachment of my transport seemed fitting. An EMT riddled me with questions to test my mental acuity, but I wasn't much interested in proving myself.

"What day of the week is it?" they asked.

Are you serious right now? I thought. I can mess that one up on a good day, but today I could not even pretend to care.

My view of the outside world was tiny. The postage-stamp windows of this hearse were my only aperture. I lay still, eyes fixed on those little panes of cloudy light as the ambulance pulled from my drive. We maneuvered onto the road, and the most unexpected array of color began to fill those little windows—a rainbow. My entire worldview in that moment was filled with the sign of His promise. His presence, His peace in my storm, became palpable. I couldn't unsee it. Maybe hope wasn't lost. Maybe this wasn't what I feared most after all.

In the midst of our greatest pain, His fingerprints, His peace, are still all over our lives.

Past Understanding

Last summer I sat watching Tyler, now fourteen, swim competitively for our local swim team. Darkness closed in on the pool of this nearby community and the meet dragged on. Swim meets can last long into the night, and it was often our protocol for the younger kids to go home with Ross while I stayed and cheered Tyler on. Most of the fans must have had bedtimes similar to my younger kids, because the bleachers, stationed a few feet outside the pool fencing, were sparse now. Only the spectators who *had* to be there were left—parents waiting for the final relays to wrap up so they could take their swimmers home. I sat alone.

That's when I noticed him. Disheveled and unkept, he was the kind who stands out, catches your eye, for all the wrong reasons. He made his way up the almost-empty bleachers, straight toward me, and proceeded to sit right in front of me, a row ahead. He was fidgeting anxiously, his body in continual motion, and repeatedly he turned around to eye me over his left shoulder. My heart began racing faster than the competing swimmers I was there to watch, and I began to wonder if this was how *Dateline* stories began.

He sat, and I worried. And then he suddenly got up and walked away. My heart rate steadied, and I began breathing again as I kept a wary eye on his whereabouts. Oddly enough, he seemed to be doing the same—continually peeking back at me through his wild curls as he walked away. So bizarre.

A few minutes later, he returned. Same seat, same restlessness, same eyeing me over his shoulder. I started talking to God this time. Not out loud, of course, but in my mind the full conversation began.

What do I do, God? I can't leave. Tyler is here. Should I go stand, unknown and uninvited, by that group of people in lawn chairs? How do I get out of here without walking closer to him? Is he going to reach out and grab me?

In my conversation, my heart rate immediately slowed, and I knew I was going to be okay.

This is where you should know, I'm not a feeler. Action almost always trumps feelings in my book, and my instincts tend to follow. Every personality test I have ever taken confirms this. I once had an instructor, who was giving me the breakdown on my personality test results, tell me I had the emotions of a male CEO. To this day I don't really know what this means, but I interpret it as (A) not all that flattering, and (B) I'm not all that emotional and feely. However, in this moment, on those bleachers, it was different.

The peace I felt was so strong, even this male CEO-type could not ignore it. *I was okay.* I stared down what scared me, turned my eyes, and talked to God about it. And He answered. *Stay awake, Katie. I got this.* The message could not have been more clear.

It might sound bizarre, but then, peace that surpasses all understanding *would*, right? The New Living Translation conveys Paul's famous words to the Philippians as follows:

Don't worry about anything; instead, pray about everything. Tell God what you need, and thank him for all he has done. Then you will experience God's peace, which exceeds anything we can understand. His peace will guard your hearts and minds as you live in Christ Jesus. (Philippians 4:6–7)

In Psalm 25, David tells us this:

The LORD confides in those who fear him; he makes his covenant known to them. My eyes are ever on the LORD, for only he will release my feet from the snare. (Psalm 25:14–15 NIV)

Both Paul and David are talking about the same thing in different contexts. When we take our eyes off what is in front of us, real and scary as that may be, when we reorient our fear toward God and cast our cares on Him, as Peter says, whether or not our immediate circumstances visibly change, peace that doesn't even make sense will not only reign, but keep, guard, and protect us. I don't know about you, friend, but I desperately need peace beyond what I can even make sense of when hope seems lost, when situations feel really, truly scary, and my thoughts want to run wild in every direction. I need His peace to guard my heart and mind here.

My actions on the bleachers that night, or lack thereof, probably contradict the advice of most self-defense wisdom, but stay with me. I'm not dishing out defense advice, I'm just telling you how it went down. I was studying the fear of God intently that particular summer, and God taught me something here. He provided peace that brought clarity of thought and heart and mind.

The unusual man in front of me got up and walked away again, and I didn't let him out of my sight until a woman I didn't know surprised me from the other side. "Is that man making you uncomfortable?" Her question was clear, direct.

"Um, yes."

Where did she come from? How had she noticed?

"Okay. I know the police chief. I'll give him a call."

That was all she said, and she was gone.

Within minutes the police arrived, and we learned that this mentally ill man was well-known to local authorities. That knowledge was interesting to me. And potentially helpful as my husband and I discussed different ways I could wisely read and navigate a similar situation in the future.

However, none of that information was as helpful as realizing what, exactly, I fear most. I may have been physically unprepared that night, possibly even naive, but spiritually I knew exactly what to do. Nothing compares to the peace that comes from fearing God more than what is in front of me. *Dateline* jokes aside, the thought of death really did cross my mind. *What if it's a gun he is fidgeting with in his pocket? What if it really is me he is after? What if something really bad happens here?*

You and I have both read enough news stories to know these thoughts weren't outside the realm of possibility. And the real answer to my every question in that moment was not a heart that beat faster, trembling hands, or teary eyes—it was peace. I was overcome with palpable peace in that situation—peace that He is good regardless, even if. This is none other than the fear of the Lord.

Now will peace be palpable in every situation? I'm not saying that. I'm not telling you to pray in real and scary places until you get a warm and fuzzy feeling and God sends someone to fix it. Don't read that. But what I *am* saying is that when things get scary, our focus gets narrow. Hands cupped around the eyes, remember? We zero in and that's all we see. But Jesus had more to say about that:

> These things I have spoken to you while I am still with you. But the Helper, the Holy Spirit, whom the Father will send in my name, he will teach you all things and bring to your remembrance all that I have said to you. Peace I leave with you; my peace I give to you. Not as the world gives do I give to you. Let not your hearts be troubled, neither let them be afraid. (John 14:25–27 NASB)

The word for *afraid* here, *deiliaō*, is unique. It is never used in a positive sense, a fear-of-God sense, but rather speaks to timidity and fearfulness. As Jesus tells of the gift of His peace, this fearfulness is what He is remedying. And He tells us the Holy Spirit is our teacher; He will call into memory, help us focus in on these very words of Christ for all who believe.

Peace is the gift in His absence here on earth. Peace is the offering in the face of what would otherwise churn our hearts, trouble us, scare us. The Holy Spirit is the Helper who teaches and reminds and offers peace.

Just now I paused my writing and went upstairs. How timely that my eleven-year-old daughter, Bailey, would be playing that very cup-your-hands-around-your-eyes game. She sized up my 5'5" frame from across the room and then held out her fingers only an inch or two apart. "Mama," she declared, smiling widely, "you're only this tall!"

What if walls closing in, tunnel vision, is a gift of clarity? Stare wide-eyed into fear and the diagnosis is large, the grief is expansive, the hole you need to dig your marriage out of is vast. But when those walls do close in and your focus narrows, hands cupped around your eyes, distraction fades. Your view is smaller. Now prompted by the Holy Spirit, your Helper-reminder, you can choose to turn your eyes toward Jesus. His peace, His greatness fills the whole tunnel, your entire worldview, like the rainbow—my visible reminder of His promise in the ambulance.

Could our hurt, our fear, be an opportunity to see Him more fully, trust Him more completely, let Him fill our narrow focus? Jesus said, "This is the only work God wants from you: Believe in the one he has sent" (John 6:29 NLT). What if fear is the fertile soil to grow faith, to believe and trust and know and fill our view with the One He has sent?

Pam Rosewell Moore, caretaker for Corrie ten Boom in the final years of her life, reflects on Corrie's wisdom in *The Five Silent Years of Corrie ten Boom*. She recounts how in a conversation with Corrie she came to the very realization of what we are discussing here. Corrie told her, "Pam, you have got to learn to see great things great and small things small." Pam writes, "I thought of these things daily in the light of a new and awesome awareness of God's sovereignty, I found that I was beginning to learn to look more and more in the right direction, and as I did so, I started to see things in a more correct perspective."[1]

Do you see that she is alluding to vertical versus horizontal fear? Direction changes perspective. When we lock eyes with Christ in our fear, when we choose to fear Him as greater, fully worthy of our adoration, faith is the by-product. Peace amid the hard is the by-product. May we have the courage to pursue Him in the storm, lock eyes with the One worth fearing, and know Him more on the other side.

CHAPTER 11

Worship

If our knowledge of God is superficial, our worship will be superficial.

R.C. Sproul

The quiet question that lingered from my teenage years—*how do people survive these things?*—now pulsed loud, demanded an answer.

How do you breathe when your baby can't? How do you endure being medicinally forced back into labor to finish a job your body won't—when plan A becomes plan B, C, and D, and now you're wheeled back to an operating room? How do you find words when a funeral director visits your hospital bed and asks you questions you can't possibly have answers to? Peace in the storm steadies our steps, but life requires that we must keep stepping. A response is necessary.

In the shifting of all we fear, our eyes firmly fixed on the only One worthy, the revelation of who He is here, now, even in hard seasons, predicates, necessitates, worship. It is our natural response to knowing Him, seeing Him.

I've seen people make this connection gracefully, instinctively almost, in hard times. I wasn't one of them. My reflexes in grief and disappointment, thick and foggy emotions that were novel to me, clouded my seeing and knowing. I had so many questions for the God I *said* I trusted, the God I *wanted* to trust. The pain and hurt of real challenges and real life can trick us into discounting God's goodness when our limited worldview speaks otherwise. That's exactly where I was when I finally knelt at my church altar and poured out tears and complaints David-style. I whispered the words with all seriousness, "I feel like no one understands, like *you* don't understand." And they echoed back in my head. *I feel like He doesn't understand the pain of separation, the death of a child? Really? Who do I believe He is?*

In *Systematic Theology*, Wayne Grudem discusses worship as an "outpouring of our hearts in response to a realization of who God is" and "the natural response of the believing heart to a clear awareness of God's presence and character."[1]

That informal definition is comprised from the whole of what we see in Scripture and specifically what we learn in Matthew 14:33 and Hebrews 12:28–29 respectively:

> Then the disciples worshiped him. "You really are the Son of God!" they exclaimed.[2]

> Since we are receiving a Kingdom that is unshakable, let us be thankful and please God by worshiping him with holy fear and awe. For our God is a devouring fire.[3]

If fear leads us to the knowledge of God, then worship is a natural by-product of knowing and loving Him. It is what we are compelled to do when we catch a glimpse of who He is, His greatness, splendor, and overwhelming love for us. Worship is the only appropriate response.

It's what I felt, what I could barely even put words to, when His rainbow filled the ambulance window. It's the meekness of us meeting the magnanimity of Him, humility glimpsing pure greatness. It's awareness of His engagement and even a tiny understanding of His worthiness. It's responsive. It's worship.

Our Response

Worship was Moses' response at the burning bush and Joshua's response to the angel of the Lord. Worship was the disciples' response when Jesus stepped on that boat, calming the storm after Peter walked on the water toward Him, and worship was the response of the woman who shattered the perfume bottle and tenderly washed Jesus' feet.[4] Don't let familiarity soften the difficulty of those stories for you. We know Moses was scared, Joshua was standing face to face with sword-drawn opposition, and that woman was under ridicule for the extent of her elaborate gift. These were believers compelled to worship at the sight of the God they knew, loved, and feared. Their worship was a chosen response.

In the Psalms, we have already caught a diary-like peek into David's heart of worship and his raw and intimate methods of pursuing Christ, regardless of his current circumstances. This isn't situational worship—it's Sunday morning at 9:30 and the piano is playing, so worship is what we do—this is worship gutted out in the truth of who God is, *regardless* of our situation and the time and a piano. This is *fearing Him* regardless, because our situations do not change the truth of who He is.

Let that sink in a minute, friend, because it is not easy. This is worshiping God for who He is when you meet the love of your life, and worshiping God when you long so badly to be married, but that does not appear to be the path God has for you right now. This is worshiping God when new life grows in your belly and still worshiping when the barrenness of that belly rips your heart raw. It's worshiping Him when diagnoses come and marriage hurts. It's worshiping Him when relationships gut you, you get overlooked for the promotion, and you're stuck where you never wanted to be.

The effects of every one of these situations is real. The emotions that come with these realities are intense. And yet not a single one changes the truth of who God is.

So in order to worship, heart overflowing, shattered, or scarred, we have to shift our gaze, lift our eyes. Just as we are learning to reorient our fears, we must also reorient our affections. Yes, this process is easier some days than others, but the work is not in producing an outcome; it's in focusing our gaze, locking eyes with Jesus rather than on the swirling world around us.

I love the example we have of this in Psalm 56:3. The verse is classic, "When I am afraid, I will trust in You." It seems like a short and sweet prescriptive, one we should jot down and say on repeat. But when we look at it in context, dig a little deeper, we learn more of the grit. Here are a few things worth noticing:

(1) David was speaking from the trenches. He was not holed up in a lofty tower penning encouragement to the lowly who were struggling with their daily battles. *He was in it.*

The verses prior, Psalm 56:1–2, say, "Be merciful to me, O God, for man would swallow me up; fighting all day he oppresses me. My enemies would hound me all day, for there are many who fight against me, O Most High." Do you get a sense of the real scene and setting here? David was in over his head, living a *how do people survive this* moment. And in *that* place, begging for mercy and under intense oppression, he directed his eyes to the Most High and took his stand.

(2) He was making a better battle plan. He wasn't pretending it wasn't messy, he was bossing himself around while he was knee deep in it. Please don't skip over this, friend. More than ever, as can-do women we are becoming experts at minimizing our hard. We are convinced this is a mind game, someone else has it harder, and we really need to get over ourselves. While there is a vein of truth in that, the end result of this way of thinking is not all that helpful—because there has to be a way to acknowledge the reality of life's challenges for what they are, and because our response to this method of minimizing our frustrations and fears is actually applying more of *us* rather than more of what we know to be the *real* Source of our hope and peace. Do you see that? Rather than seeing hard things for what they are and then bringing them to Jesus, we get stuck talking ourselves out of them. We're choosing Band-Aids and mind games over real faith and real healing.

In Romans 4:19, Paul talked Abraham up for grasping this understanding. I love how the NIV states it: "Without weakening in his faith, he faced the fact that his body was as good as dead—since he was about a hundred years old—and that Sarah's womb was also dead."

Do you see that? Face the facts, without weakening in your faith. That was Abraham's M.O., and David's too.

David established a "When this, then that" battle plan. "*When* I am afraid—yes, I'm scared, this is messy and hard—*then* I will trust in you—I will reorient my eyes, my heart, my worship toward you, Lord." David was commanding himself to focus on truth.

(3) He reminded himself of what is true and declared it. The passage goes on, "You number my wanderings; put my

tears into Your bottle . . . this I know because God is for me" (vv. 8–9). David had some history with God. Two months or twenty-five years in, so do you. On top of that, you have the canon of Scripture, the history of God's faithfulness since creation, and the testimony of the saints around you. In the throes of life, you must remind yourself of who God is and declare it. This is worship.

(4) He humbled himself to worship: "I will render praise to you. For you have delivered my soul from death. Have you not kept my feet from falling" (vv. 12–13). Do you see exactly where David's remembrance and declaration of truth led him? To praise and worship. The reality of David's circumstances did not change one tiny bit between these few verses, but the reality of his heart did.

This is the invitation for you and me. David's God has not changed. This is our God. This is why we fleshed out the immutability of God early on, because we have to read this and know that this truth is for us today. Our unchanging God inhabits the praise of His people. He works in and amid our pain when we choose to lock eyes with Him and fear Him even here, even in what we consider our worst fears.

I wish I could say that was a straight line for me. After I gave birth to my perfectly formed, lifeless daughter, I wanted the physical and emotional healing to be immediate, linear, quick. I'm guessing you have wanted the same in your pain and fears too?

I wanted Jesus to step into the boat, walk through my storm, and calm the wind and waves not momentarily, but permanently. The work of grief is slow and messy. The work of hurt and healing takes time, but worship in these places is a hallowed-out offering from our emptiest parts, bravely asking Him to fill them with more of himself. It's raw, cut open, and His Word, His touch, feels nearer than we may ever experience otherwise.

Turning our eyes to Him in hurt is the most beautiful and intimate experience of our lives. It can be our deepest, most pressing form of worship—and our bravest.

Learn to fear Him here, friend. Stand on truth with wobbly legs and a tear-stained face and see, maybe for the first time, the strength and courage, the bravery, that only He can give. He is good and near, here. Fear Him. Worship Him. Allow the change to begin inside of you, in your heart, in your adoration and affections, before it even meets your circumstances. This is the specialty of our Helper—fear, peace, worship—eyes rightly aligned to the only One worthy.

CHAPTER 12

Hope

She offered herself honestly and beautifully, sharing something from within her laced with courage and hope.

Emily P. Freeman, A Million Little Ways:
Uncover the Art You Were Made to Live

We named her Alison Joline, and weeks after she was gone, I still felt the flutter of her movement inside of me. There is probably some technical term for those ghost feelings. I won't try to impress you by pretending to know it, Googling so I can set it here all smart-like. Sometimes we know terms at a heart-level long before we learn the proper jargon. It was like the phantom vibration of a cell phone ring we have all jumped for a time or two, but this wasn't a missed call. This was a missed life, my heart breaking all over again. I wanted every gurgle of my tummy to be her. I wanted the doctors to be wrong. Sometimes I almost convinced myself they were.

One afternoon I tucked myself into the oversized leather recliner in our sunroom and let my mind spin and drift. I couldn't puzzle out the events I had lived in the past few days, few months. The finality didn't make sense to me so I just thought harder. *Maybe if I think hard enough, I can fix this? There must be a loophole they missed, something the doctors forgot.* For a moment, I began to believe if I thought hard enough, I could defy hurt, defy death, right it all.

It makes no sense and yet perfect sense if you have ever been in a situation you didn't want to be in, a situation that wasn't supposed to be that way.

We've actually been trained to respond this way, pivoting for a quick plan B, haven't we? Think about it. From about two years old, probably even earlier, we start to understand that the world is not going to work precisely the way we want it to. We want candy and we don't always get it. We don't like vegetables and we have to eat them anyway. We don't get to play with keys or remotes or maybe phones, even though they are much more fascinating than the wooden blocks that are handed to us. The world that was all yeses as an infant—people jumping in response to our every cry—becomes increasingly full of no's.

It's not an easy gig, learning the no, and our will revolts in physical and obvious ways. We scream, shout, and throw ourselves down in a show of our earnest displeasure at the disappointment.

As a mom of four, I've done some time teaching and training through these tricky years. As a thirty-nine-year-old woman, I've spent quite a few years *learning* through them. While I'm fully convinced this training and learning is important, essential even, there is a part of me, with my grown-up frustrations and disappointments, that can look at a two-year-old and say, "Oh, girl, I get it. I so get it."

111

I know you get it too.

But we wisely work hard to teach the next generation to adapt. Not this, but that. No mud in your hair, but sure, mud on your hands. No ice cream for breakfast, but yes, after dinner. No friend over today, but yes, next week. We raise some great adapters just as our mamas did.

As we age, our skills only improve. We become even better adapters in increasingly complex disappointments. Okay, not him, but maybe someone else. Okay, not marriage now, but maybe later. Okay, maybe no kids right now, not that job right now, not that body right now, not that relationship with my spouse right now, but maybe *someday*.

And that works well, until it doesn't. Until the time runs out, until the pain breaks us, the disappointment breaks us, and we can't be happy-talked into believing that something equally appeasing is just around the corner. The logic fails and we wrap ourselves into that leather recliner parked in the sunroom and cry tears that burn inside and out.

Hope as a result of our own adaptability isn't durable enough. Life is simply too tough, too unsteady, too painful for that. Eventually we reach our elastic limit. We meet a place we simply can't snap back from.

This is the bottom I had to reach to begin to see Him clearly, to see all of the places my faith was based on outcomes and my solution was more of me. Yes, as a lifelong believer, I knew how to pray. I knew how to read Scripture and even quote a handful of the really good ones. But this is where I began to know God in a completely different way. This is where I found a hope that did not disappoint. It wasn't a light switch, a one-and-done moment, but it was a spark—the beginning of understanding hope beyond my circumstances. Psalm 147 makes me think the Lord was patiently waiting for me to get there all along:

He does not delight in the strength of the horse; he takes no pleasure in the legs of a man. The LORD takes pleasure in those who fear Him, in those who hope in His mercy. (Psalm 147:10–11)

When hope shifts from outcomes and results, to the person of Jesus Christ, we will finally find ourselves on solid ground.

The Hope of Glory

In the book of Romans, commonly referred to as the Constitution of the Christian religion, Paul outlined how this hope-filled process works:

Having been justified by faith, we have peace with God through our Lord Jesus Christ, through whom also we have access by faith in this grace in which we stand and rejoice in hope of the glory of God. And that not only that, but we also glory in tribulations, knowing that tribulation produces perseverance and perseverance, character and character, hope. Now hope does not disappoint, because the love of God has been poured out in our hearts by the Holy Spirit who was given to us. (Romans 5:1–5)

Hope that doesn't disappoint can feel like a unicorn to any of us who have lived long with our feet on the ground. On some level, we've all hoped and been disappointed. We have wanted and wished and worked for outcomes. We have prayed and pled and petitioned. And in a million different ways, big or small, we've delivered stillborn dreams, shattered hopes that leave scars. But Paul is teaching us about something different in this passage. *How?* Let's crack open his words and see what we find. Romans 5 is set up by the previous chapter, which tells us of Abraham's profound faith—faith, we are told over and over, that was credited to him as righteous. His belief in God—not only in who He was, but what He would, in fact, do, regardless of Abraham's present circumstances, was straight up righteousness. That should get our attention, friend. Our belief, our faith, regardless of how hard or scary or ridiculous the mountain or desert in front of us is, matters.

So Paul meets us with that intro, and in chapter 5 tells us that the faith that justifies us also affords us peace with God. We're building on where we just came from in the last chapter now, aren't we? We have access, we stand in grace, and we get to rejoice in the hope of His glory. This makes Paul's command to the church in Philippi to "rejoice in all things" make sense, right? Paul was in prison when he wrote those words. He wasn't pulling out some happy talk; he bone-deep *knew* the hope of glory that he is telling us about.

But that's not all: Paul tells us we also get to rejoice in the hard stuff, our problems, trials, sufferings, because that work produces perseverance. This is the quiet and unseen fruit growing here. Perseverance—steadfastness amid opposition, brave patience. The ability to keep trusting when loneliness won't quit, when we're so long overlooked, misunderstood, ignored. The ability to keep serving when motherhood is hard and that teenager is wholly ungrateful. The ability to be true to our vows and keep loving when our marriage is stale and the future is not bright. The ability to see the real challenge right in front of you, to be weary and exhausted from the long battle, and defiantly keep right on going.

We have to know this is possible. We have to grasp this, have the grit to look beyond the instantaneous, the frivolous and filtered world we scroll through and say—this is worth it, this is good, because God is growing something beautiful and rich here and I don't stand alone. No wonder Paul started with faith, right? He knew we were going to need it.

But he's far from done. That grit will in turn produce character, experience, a track record with God. It will root you deep in the knowledge of who He is and what He has done before your very eyes. He will begin to build a heritage in and through you, one story at a time. This is incredible. This is what He does in you, through you. And that character, that proving, results in hope. *Vine's Complete Expository Dictionary* calls that confident expectation having to do with the unseen and future.[1]

This all begins to make sense, doesn't it? It's full circle. Because we *know*, we get to walk through trials with a new lens. This doesn't mean it doesn't hurt. Of course not. But devastating disappointment does not have to lead to destruction. Our destruction is the devil's business and we don't have to give him that ground, even in our deepest hurt.

You can bet I cried every day for weeks after saying good-bye to Alison. Sometimes the tears still come when my mind wanders to what might have been, to what my family might look like with an Ali Jo in the mix. I imagine she would have been my only child with my brown eyes. Her early fight would probably make her a spunky competitor, both a frustration and friend to her barely-a-year-older brother, a little mama to her three younger siblings. These dreams still ache in me at times. That's real.

But I can hold that truth in the same wide open hands, the same wide open heart that knows God has grown and still is growing good there because *He is good there.* He has healed and is healing, and seeing Him there has produced a defiant hope in me—a forged hope, refined through fire and able to trust Him beyond what I see in front of me at the moment. Living this out is not perfect by any means, but knowing bone-deep that He really is the hope that does not disappoint affords courage that nothing else in this world ever could. The psalmist affirmed this truth when he wrote, "The eye of the Lord is on those who fear Him, on those who hope in His mercy" (Psalm 33:18).

His eyes on us, our hope in His mercy, His kindness, His unfailing love. This is it, friend. This is the beautiful opportunity that pain, tribulation in Paul's words, affords.

Paul rounds out that Romans 5 selection on triumphant faith with these words:

> Now hope does not disappoint, because the love of God has been poured out in our hearts by the Holy Spirit who was given to us. (v. 5)

Proverbs 23 puts it this way:

> Don't let your heart envy sinners; instead, always fear the LORD. For then you will have a future, and your hope will not be dashed. (vv. 17–18 CSB)

To fear God is to know and understand Him. To know Him is to live confidently in His love poured out by His Holy Spirit, our Comforter, Helper. And it is in *this* place that we live with real hope, hope that will never disappoint us even when circumstances do.

We don't serve outcomes or hope in outcomes, we serve God. We trust He is good, we honor Him as worthy, and plant our hope in His sovereignty and faithful goodness. This is a firm foundation, friend. A sure footing that affords courage even when the storm rages. This is the soil in which real bravery begins to grow. And as we choose to pursue Him, to fear Him here, we can begin to pray:

> *Be near, O Lord, in our hurt and hope. Lift our eyes, invade our desire, make us more like you. We believe, we trust. Give us holy courage to place our hope in you alone. Be our all.*

CHAPTER 13

Humility

Part of humility means trusting God with our plans and submitting to the possibility that they will not be fulfilled.

Hannah Anderson, Humble Roots:
How Humility Grounds and Nourishes Your Soul

The most difficult question we ask in pain is, *"Why?"* Why me? Why now? Why this? What possible good could come from this, God?

I turned a sideways eye to the pregnant teens I saw anywhere, everywhere. A robust and healthy, unplanned, maybe even unwanted child growing inside of her while my empty body and heart bled the loss. On my ugliest days I sneered at God covertly. *Really?*

Our life-long learning of who God is makes the *why* questions even more difficult. We fully believe He can write a different story for us. It is in His power to do so. We don't doubt He is able. But sometimes He doesn't. And that pain can rattle us more deeply than the loss itself.

I could recite the truths I learned in Sunday school with surety. *Yes, I believe you are all knowing. Yes, I believe you are all powerful and you are everywhere. I believe you love wildly, more than I can even comprehend.* But what's a girl to do when the truth she believes does not match up with the reality she holds in her hands, the hurt that robs her oxygen?

The same question has reverberated through the ages in all of our gutted moments—*God, you are good, but why does it feel like you are not good to me?*

We convince ourselves that this question is original, solo, but our communal ability to resonate with the heart behind it denies that very belief. Even so, God is gracious to give us evidence of this ache repeatedly in Scripture.

Think of Hannah, broken and bitter because of her barren womb and the shame her husband's other wife lobbed at her continually. Hannah didn't eye the other pregnant women with envy from a distance as I did. She was *living with* the worst of the mean girls, who, from her own disappointment, took pleasure in exposing Hannah's wounds, prodding them. This is a story line made for reality television.

Though Elkanah, Hannah's husband, loved Hannah wildly and displayed that obviously, it wasn't enough, and her inability to become a mother consumed and wrecked her.

We know that too, don't we? We suffer blindness to the good and perfect gifts we have already been given, become incapable of comprehending them, let alone enjoying them, as we fixate on what we don't have. What we *believe* is best for us. What seems available to all the world around us and yet specifically withheld from us.

I bounced Tyler, my now-eighteen-month-old, healthy boy on my hip with this incredulity plaguing my heart. The desire for what I didn't have, couldn't have, became a cancer for what I did have. I pretended it didn't exist, let it grow unattended, and allowed it to atrophy my faith in quiet and unseen places.

Hannah, in this same cancerous place, desperate from years of this hurt, did the only thing she knew. She arrived before the Lord of hosts at Shiloh, as Matthew Henry says, in "humility and holy shamefacedness."[1] Her lips moved silently before God. This woman knew what pain that robs your oxygen, grief that comes out as worship, prayer without sound, feels like. Varying translations give us a collective description of our friend Hannah in 1 Samuel 1:10—she wept bitterly, she wept in anguish, wept with many tears. She wept sore.

But there she was. She did not wrap herself in a catacomb of pain, stay home to grow the scar tissue of acrid bitterness in isolation. She presented herself before the Lord, as would have been her annual spiritual practice. She showed up, a mess, and she spilled it.

What I love most about Hannah's story, more than the end result of Samuel, is that in her humility, God met her. *Before* she became a mother, *before* Scripture even tells us she slept with her husband, Hannah left the temple changed. This woman who refused food now ate. The woman who had just wept sore a few verses before was now visibly free from the sadness that had been her cloak. The years of disappointment, doubt, and disbelief that Hannah had battled alone, the disillusionment that had riddled deep into her countenance was lifted, not because of an outcome, but because she met the Lord of hosts. *The state of Hannah's situation had not changed; the state of her heart did.*

Humility is another by-product of fearing the Lord, more fruit of holy fear. When we catch a glimpse of who God is, rightly align our fear and affections to Him, we cannot help but be humbled in His presence and be changed.

Arrogance is almost inherent today, particularly in Western culture. Living with a certain amount of health, wealth, and freedom threads deep in us expectation and assumptions we are barely even aware of. It is woven into the fabric of the way we exist. I live a whopping twenty miles from where I was born, and my minimal travel in these thirty-nine years gives me little experience with which to address the complexity of these issues. However, even this small-town girl can pick up her Bible and see the elephant of arrogance and entitlement in the room.

Get a high school diploma and you earn the expectation of college. Get a college diploma and you earn the expectation of a high-paying job. Get a job and you earn the expectation of a nice house in a good neighborhood. Or perhaps the expectation of marriage and kids. Not only do we make plans, we bank on our own culturally influenced expectations of the way our life *should* go. Our arrogance is as palpable as our frustration when we don't get what we want, hoped for, planned for, expected.

Seeing how we got here is not nearly as helpful as choosing what we do once we *are* here. Hannah made a choice to bow and pursue vulnerability and humility in her hurt, her honest pouring out, her "depth of anguish and resentment," her "great anxiety and vexation," her "abundance of complaint and grief." At the risk of overstating the point, I think it's essential that we flesh out the depths of Hannah's hurt, because when we read the story fast in full, when we remember the retelling from our childhood, we often fail to pause in the pain. We know how the story ends and it's easy to minimize Hannah's story to a Disney fairy tale that it is not. The messy middle matters. Hannah humbled herself before God, and baby or no baby, He changed her. This is our God. Humbling ourselves is what it means to fear Him.

How do we get there? When pain and disappointment leave us gasping for air and running for shelter, drawing ourselves inward for refuge and protection, how do we move toward humility?

We do what we know. As we have discussed, much of how we respond in pain, in hurt, and in disappointment is reflexive. Truths we have believed in the off-season, every moment of our lives leading up to now, begin to surface.

Think about it: A superlative nature is reflexive to us. When we are annoyed at friends and family, people we love, for their less favorable attributes, we do this: "She *always* . . . bails, takes advantage, makes it about her." Is this true? Probably not, at least not *always*, but when we are disappointed or frustrated, our past experience bolts to the surface and we let our emotions proclaim it as fact.

A good counselor will help us nip this superlative rhetoric quickly. But the fact remains that what we quietly believe about the people we love rises to the surface, gets tested quickly, when things get hard.

The same can be said of our relationship with God. What we know of Him, who we know Him to be, rushes to the surface when we are hurt. Whether our understanding of Him is weak or robust, we put it all on trial something fast in tough times. How we are invested in Him now, today, matters more than we know. And knowing Him will always result in humility. But what is humility exactly? I'm glad you asked.

Humility Is Proper Positioning

We are called to submit ourselves both to God and others as an act of humility produced by godly fear. Do I even need to tell you this is not a popular concept today? Though our culture applauds independence and autonomy, we cannot argue with the clear instruction of Scripture.

After teaching the elders about proper leadership, Peter said:

> In the same way, you who are younger, be subject to the elders.
> All of you clothe yourselves with humility toward one another,
> because *God resists the proud but gives grace to the humble.*
> *Humble yourselves, therefore, under the mighty hand of God,*
> so that he may exalt you at the proper time, casting all your
> cares on him, because he cares about you. (1 Peter 5:5–7 CSB,
> emphasis added)

Likewise, Paul instructed the church at Ephesus to "submit
to one another in the fear of God" (Ephesians 5:21).

Do you see Hannah's example between the lines here? She
knew this truth long before these words were written, and in
the midst of deep pain she *believed* them, *lived* them.

She had no idea what the "proper time" Peter spoke of would
look like. Chances are, if it were up to her, that proper time
would have been a *long* time before. *Oh, Hannah, we get you.*
But she submitted her will to God. She came before Him a
complete mess of hurt and tears. She knew, even in her grief,
that the answer to her pain would be found in humility, pouring
out her soul before her God.

Hannah left the weight of her burden with Him, and He
answered. She was changed by the proper position of her heart's
desire, not by the outcome. That is beautiful.

Humility Is All Eyes on God

Humility is a one-on-one game that may be unseen by the world
around us but is born first and foremost out of a proper relationship with Christ. Anything less results in more pride, more
of us. *Do you see that?*

Paul instructed the church in Ephesus in this very thing. He exhorted them to pursue wisdom and cheer each other on by speaking the Word, singing together, giving thanks, and "submitting to one another in the fear of God."

Our healthy relationship to others is born out of a proper fear of God. This is the beginning of wisdom, how we live wisely in this world. Why wouldn't it start here?

> Bondservants, obey your earthly masters with fear and trembling, with a sincere heart, as you would Christ, not by the way of eye-service, as people-pleasers, but as bondservants of Christ, doing the will of God from the heart, rendering service with a good will as to the Lord and not to man. (Ephesians 6:5–7 ESV)

How do we treat others well? We fear God and let that submission overflow to those around us. This is the product not simply of conformed actions, but of a transformed heart. We have all seen this, in our kids, friends, those whom we do life with. We know the difference between transformed actions and a transformed heart. So does God.

Keep your eyes on Him. Fear Him here and let that humility pour out into every other relationship you have.

Humility Is Being Teachable

From the dawn of creation, we humans have loved to *know*. Our sinful nature hungers and thirsts for it. Satan chose his words wisely: "Your eyes will be opened, and you will be like God, knowing good and evil."[2] The realization of how much we *know* is repulsive to many of us now. Read the news; the knowing is ugly. And yet at the same time we keep filling shelves, trading our hard-earned cash for stacks of self-help tomes. Spending hours scrolling through photos of other peoples' lives on our tiny screens. We want to know.

Humility is more languid and slow. It is learning as much as knowing. It is process and engagement. God meets our humble hunger and agrees in Scripture to teach us:

> Who, then, are those who fear the LORD? He will instruct them in the ways they should choose. (Psalm 25:12 NIV)

> Teach me your way, O LORD, that I may walk in your truth; unite my heart to fear your name. (Psalm 86:11 ESV)

The inverse is also true. God speaks to the Israelites through the prophet Jeremiah and warns us of what happens when we are not teachable:

> They have not been humbled to this day, nor have they feared; they have not walked in My law or in My statutes that I set before you and your fathers. (Jeremiah 44:10)

Humility speaks loudly of relationship, of being teachable as we learn more of who God is and who we are in light of that. Fearing God is the beginning of knowing Him, and knowing Him produces an innate humility. Humility unites our hearts to fear His name. Full circle.

We are called to humility—to our God and toward others, in the fear of Him. This is not natural and it is not what the world sells. From lipstick ads to the sports figures we love to cheer for, humility is not the currency of our culture. But it is the currency of Christ, it is the fruit that sets us apart. It is proper positioning and a righteous understanding of our solid identity in Him. May it be so. In fear of the only One worthy, may we overflow with humility and boldly shine *His* light, that in us the world will see more of Him.

CHAPTER 14

Heritage

Only as God graciously opens our eyes to his glory and captures our hearts with his awe will we ever be his instruments in the eyes of our children.

Paul David Tripp, Awe: Why It Matters
for Everything We Think, Say, & Do

My husband has been telling me for years now that spontaneous times are often the best times. He heard someone say it on talk radio once and it resonated with him. The logic goes something like this—occasions we plan and prepare for can be beautiful, but the less planned and prepared moments, the ones that catch us by surprise or come without advanced notice, greet us without the weight of expectation and have the ability to become the most striking memories. At least when it comes to my godly heritage, I'm convinced he is right.

My earliest memories in the church were of my dad at the pulpit. Always. I've been gone from home for more than two decades now and my dad has been retired from regular pastoral ministry for about as long. Even so, I'm sure I'll never hear more sermons from the lips of any other preacher than I have my own father. I know how he prays and how he sings. I know the stories he tells and how he tells them. In all his sermons and all his prayers, many I've bore witness to and even more I haven't, I watched, front row, a faithful heritage paved on my behalf. And I'm grateful. But it's the more unique and spontaneous expressions of faithfulness that have branded that heritage deep into my awareness.

In the earliest days of my pregnancy, when I woke up blood-soaked and proceeded to pass out in the bathroom, Ross made two quick phone calls—one to 9-1-1 and one to my parents. The paramedics arrived first on the scene and were making sure I was stabilized by the time my parents got there. I never heard their arrival. My bedroom, my house, seemed full of people I didn't know asking questions I didn't have answers to. It was surreal and cloudy.

And then my dad was there. Surrounded by medical personnel still checking my pulse and blood pressure, he never halted, never even paused or asked permission before he approached. He came directly toward me, knelt beside me, laid his hands on me, and began to pray aloud. There is much that was lost on me in my hazy stupor that night, but his authoritative prayer was not. His direct request filled the entire room, filled my home, incense from a father to the Father, interceding for his own. He wasn't quick or discreet and his reflex in the middle of the unknown, the way he turned every eye in that room toward the God of heaven, whether they were looking for Him or not, in the midst of our confusion and fear, astounded me. This is my heritage, cemented in my mind. This is who my dad is to me and the kind of heritage I too want to leave for anyone the Lord places in my path. But if I'm honest, sometimes I wonder how I even get there—how do I develop that brand of boldness and confidence, that kind of faith and fear of the Lord and courage to declare it on demand and in an instant?

The interesting truth is that right now we're either growing it or we aren't. One day at a time we are laying a heritage with each of the relationships in our lives. As much as that one moment with my dad is etched in my forever memory, the preparation for that completely unexpected moment was laid in what he lived (and lives), what he believed (and yet believes) on a daily basis. That moment was less about one instance in which my dad's faith was a billboard, and more about the spiritual disciplines practiced over long and quiet years, the faith grown over a lifetime of knowing God and fearing God and learning the courage to put belief into real action on demand.

Do you see that? Heritage is a daily work of growing faith in quiet and unseen seasons. It is learning who God is and trusting Him faithfully to supply our needs and answer our questions. It's the courage to step bravely, one day at a time, in the full knowledge of who He is. It's the unnoticed work of determined dependence and chosen humility that hungers to not lose sight of His greatness, His realness, in the midst of our normal. It is a slow and long process of holding fast to the confession of our hope, without wavering, because He is faithful and we know it because we know Him.

I'm certain parenting wasn't *easy* for my dad in that moment. Or in so many moments before or since that one. But he knew how to respond in crisis because of the faith he had grown, believing and knowing God every day before that. He was building a godly heritage long before the moment it was wildly obvious. That's what we can do in our lives. We can do the simple and faithful work of knowing God here, building a faith so magnetic it can't help but spill over, a faith that we can stand on, together, when trials come.

Long after we are gone, we will leave a remnant of who we were and what we valued and loved. Those who knew us will know what we cherished and how we responded when life was hard. Scripture testifies that this declaring and sharing of our faith, this building of a godly heritage, is a blessing to be celebrated, a gift we want to pass on:

> For You, O God, have heard my vows; You have given me the heritage of those who fear Your name. (Psalm 61:5)

> One generation shall praise Your words to another, and shall declare Your mighty acts. (Psalm 145:4)

> For when he sees his children, the work of my hands within his nation, they will honor my name, they will honor the Holy One of Jacob and stand in awe of the God of Israel. (Isaiah 29:23 CSB)

We can't choose what others remember, but the sum of what we value will have an impact that outlives us.

Choosing the Story Our Lives Will Tell

The story of Ruth never gets old for me. I've studied it, listened to sermons, and read commentaries on it, and as is true of all of Scripture, there is always more to be mined.

Our key player in the first chapter of Ruth is Naomi, a wife and mom from the not-yet-famous town of Bethlehem. Naomi was an Israelite living in the time of the Judges, which is pretty much a four-hundred-year scar in the history of God's people as they abandoned the law of God. The New King James introduction to the book of Judges does not mince words: "This book could also appropriately be titled the 'Book of Failure.'" Quite the summary, right? I'm veering off course a bit here, but I want you to know *this* is the atmosphere, the season, and greater setting we're meeting Naomi in. It isn't pretty.

Due to a famine, Naomi's husband decides to move the family across the Dead Sea to the country of Moab. In the first five verses of the book of Ruth, Naomi makes this big move to a new country of new people with differing beliefs. Next thing we know, she becomes widowed, gains a couple daughters-in-law, and loses both of her sons who end up dying. Don't you love how the Bible can pack a punch in just a few verses?

The book of Ruth does not disclose its author; however, it's safe to assume it is not a woman, right? All cultural mores of that period aside, a woman would undoubtedly provide us with a few more details, a little more emotional context to this story, no? Granted, we are reading the inspired Word of God and we have everything we need to know, but I do think it's worth the effort to sit with the story just a minute more.

I'm guessing the author has the beauty of either distance or time and perspective to put those cataclysmic events into tidy little sentences for us. We all tend to do that in retrospect. I can tell you I was eight days overdue with my first baby with a smile on my face, remembering it like it was a tiny bump on the road. But when I was there, a pile of tears in my hospital bed at the end of the failed induction that was day seven, it was a mountain. And I was certain that baby was *never* coming out. Turns out, he did.

Let's put ourselves into Naomi's shoes. This roller coaster she is living is *brutal*. Yes, it's a few short verses, but that does not change the reality, the magnitude, of what Naomi is enduring.

Hearing that the Lord has visited the people of Bethlehem, once again providing food for them, Naomi decides to return to her homeland, and the famous interaction between Naomi and Ruth takes place. But again, if we temper our stride here, move a little more slowly into this good-bye, we notice something unique about Naomi.

Upon leaving, Naomi chooses to bless her daughters-in-law, saying, "Each of you go back to your mother's home. May the LORD show kindness to you as you have shown to the dead and to me" (Ruth 1:8 CSB). These are brave words. Naomi has lost everything; if she had any tendency toward codependency, this would be a fine time for it to surface. But instead, at her own increasing loss, she blesses her sons' wives, wishes them the kindness of the Lord, and bids them to stay with their families.

In response, these widowed daughters weep loudly and insist on returning to Bethlehem with her. I don't get the impression these are sympathy tears. This isn't an obligatory and flimsy, "Oh hey, yeah, sure we'll go with you." These women are gutted by their mother-in-law leaving. I might be stating the obvious here, but this isn't exactly a typical in-law relationship. These women are willing to trade the comforts of everything they have known, likely for their entire lives—family and friends, faith and tradition—for Naomi. We often think of how highly this speaks of the daughters-in-law, but think for a minute how highly this speaks of Naomi. This is a woman of strength and dignity. The honor and courage with which she has faced life up until this point have laid the foundation for this critical moment. Do you see the stones of faithfulness that are the firm foundation in a challenging season? Keep going, it gets better.

After a little more pleading, one daughter-in-law chooses to heed Naomi's words, while Ruth pushes all her chips to the center. She's all in. With a vow of both courage and honor, she speaks the famous words that I cannot neglect to repeat here:

Don't plead with me to abandon you or to return and not follow you. For wherever you go, I will go, and wherever you live,
I will live; your people will be my people, and your God will
be my God. (Ruth 1:16 CSB)

I wonder where Ruth learned this kind of courage? From
whom do you think she saw this kind of strength and candor?
She stands up for herself in the most submissive manner. She
chooses her words carefully and at a critical point makes the
choice that will change both her life and her lineage, her heritage. Brave women give rise to brave women. They set the stage,
carve the path, become the model for other women to follow
toward courage as well.

As widowed women, Naomi and Ruth return to Bethlehem,
living out the reality of Paul's words that would come long
after them: "Hard-pressed on every side, yet not crushed;
we are perplexed, but not in despair; persecuted, but not
forsaken; struck down, but not destroyed" (2 Corinthians
4:8–9). Ruth put her hands to work gleaning grain, which
was the welfare program of the time. God's providence over
the lives of these two women was abundant as they did the
next right thing. Naomi mentored Ruth. Ruth was attentive
and obedient to her mother-in-law's wisdom. God provided
a kinsman-redeemer in the form of Boaz who would not only
redeem the land, but the lineage of this entire family. Ruth
gave birth to Obed, who was the father of Jesse, who would
become the father of King David. This is the lineage of Jesus
Christ.

Do you see the pattern here, friend? It takes holy courage to
trust God amid bitter hurt, bitter hard, when life doesn't seem
fair. It takes holy courage to live out faithfulness when it's far
from easy, and even more, to trust that God will divinely inter-
cede for the good of His people. To trust a God whose story is

far bigger than we know or realize, to trust that God will only write good endings.

Naomi and Ruth were living a simple, but rarely easy, faithfulness. In their gritty and often uncomfortable courage they were building a heritage that would long outlive them. And so are we. Daily, faithfully. We're choosing the story our lives will tell, one we will pass on for better or worse. Our heritage is built in practiced preparation, asking, seeking, and knocking to know more of God and trust Him with our big and small decisions. It's a heritage that grasps how big our God is, chooses to fear Him, and lives boldly, bravely from that fear. It shows up in our speech, in the decisions we make, and quite possibly in how we choose to move in the hard, storming the gates of heaven for all the world to see when life gets rough. Those are examples that don't go unnoticed, examples that become our heritage and cause the world around us to behold our God. That's a holy heritage that comes from choosing a holy courage.

CHAPTER 15

Community

> We should not . . . think of our fellowship with other Christians
> as a spiritual luxury, an optional addition to the exercises of
> private devotion. We should recognise rather that such fel-
> lowship is a spiritual necessity, for God has made us in such
> a way.
>
> J. I. Packer, Knowing God

I wish I could tell you I engaged community perfectly, or at
least beautifully, in this season. I did neither. In grief I survived
and hid. I handled relationships messy, instinctively, and didn't
know how to do it any other way. That's what we do when we
don't know what to do, right? Without training or experience
we keep bumping into things. We learn, in often sloppy and
sometimes even hurtful ways.

All of a sudden I was a freshman in a brand-new school. *Hi, I'm Katie. I just gave birth to a stillborn. I'm new here. I don't know what to do here.*

Flowers, cards, and letters came, generous and kind expressions from people who didn't really know what to say to the girl who didn't really know what she needed to hear. An introductory newsletter was delivered from the bereaved parents club. For real. The day before I gave birth, I hadn't qualified for membership. Now I did.

It's no wonder these turn of events seemed awkward and strange. They *are* awkward and strange. Yesterday you thought you were healthy, but now the test results say you're not. Yesterday you had a husband, now you don't. Yesterday you had a plan, had a hope, had a dream, and today it's gone. That's kind of a big deal.

Church was the hardest. Go to the grocery store and you can hide a lot. No one asks, no one knows. But church is vulnerable. Your people know. You come to lay your heart bare before the Lord, to lift your eyes and worship alongside brothers and sisters, to open your ears and receive. To be loved. And it all felt like more emotion than I could publicly handle. I wanted to stay home. Alone. Sheltered. Protected. My version of safe.

I'm trusting you have been there too. Hurt and happy to hide. Convinced that shielded means solitary, that solo is safer. While there is a place for that—we know that even Jesus went to be by himself after He heard the news that John the Baptist had been murdered (see Matthew 14:13)—that is a place to visit and not stay, pause but not park. We are made for community. Scripture tells us:

> Two are better than one because they have a good reward for their efforts. For if either falls, his companion can lift him up; but pity the one who falls without another to lift him up. Also,

if two lie down together, they can keep warm; but how can one person alone keep warm? And if someone overpowers one person, two can resist him. A cord of three strands is not easily broken. (Ecclesiastes 4:9–12 CSB)

Just as our bodies have many parts and each part has a special function, so it is with Christ's body. We are many parts of one body, and we all belong to each other. (Romans 12:4–5 NLT)

There is so much beauty in these verses. We are better together. We need each other working elbow to elbow, side by side. Last week my friend Candee and I threw a fortieth birthday party for our friend Alesha. We invited forty more friends to join us in celebrating. We used real dishes, offered our best wishes, and dined. It was lovely. And after we soaked as much as we could from that evening, Candee and I, along with the help of our husbands and oldest daughters, worked late into the night washing dishes.

I have stayed up late doing dishes before. I'm guessing you probably have too. It's not always a good time. It's more of a preventative measure, a chore endured at the present in order to enjoy the gift of a clean kitchen the next morning. But this night was different. We chatted and laughed. We washed and dried and recounted our favorite parts of that day spent celebrating our friend. Long after the sun went down on that summer evening, after an already full day, we worked. Together. And it was probably the most fun I've ever had doing dishes.

The return for our efforts—work done more than twice as quickly, friendships growing stronger, recounting good memories at the same time we were making even more—was a sweet reward. In Ecclesiastes, Solomon tells us this is the beauty of community, of friendship. Of doing life together rather than alone.

But he doesn't stop there. Solomon talks about the falling and lifting of each other. He mentions both the warmth and strength a friend provides. It's interesting how physical and palpable the benefits are. We are stronger, braver together.

Solomon keeps going, steels deeper, "A cord of three strands is not easily broken." Linked together, tied to one another, we are each more durable, resilient, strong. In sweet times and hard ones, working or lifting, exhorting or strengthening, we cannot underestimate the value of community. We live and thrive in community, we catch the best (and the worst) of one another, and it's rarely easy. Simple, yes. Easy, no. Because we flawed humans do this messy.

Community Is Messy but Necessary

Last year I tutored a group of eight-year-olds in my kids' home-school co-op. Eager for all that was new on the first day of class, the energy was high as kids settled themselves into plastic chairs pulled up to pint-sized tables. There were nine of them, some I knew, most I didn't, and we were going to spend a year learning together. I had no clue how quickly, or deeply, we would dive in.

Kevin, one of my new students, had his hand up before class even officially began. His brow creased and wrinkled, his face was serious. When I acknowledged his interjection, he made his request known clearly, strongly, to the entire class: "I don't want to sit by him! Can I sit over there?"

"Him" was Brian, the sweet boy with the twisted body. Brian was tucked in his walker, parked right next to Kevin. Kevin's words hung in the air for a moment, strained silence for what felt like forever, as I grasped for a way to respond. I heard my own sharp inhale, felt it. Brian's mom was in the room, and as I shot a momentary glance her way, I saw her poker face break just a little. As uncomfortable as this moment was for me, it was acute pain for her.

I kept moving as quickly as I could, wondering if I could somehow gloss the moment over with grace and speed. "That is not a very nice thing to say, Kevin. I need you to sit right where you are. Everyone please take out your maps."

A quick reprimand and request for obedience. *Deep breaths, Katie. Just keep going.* I felt hot and unsettled. I continued teaching the class while replaying my own words in my head again and again. *Did I handle that correctly? Hi, I'm Katie. And I'm new here. Again.*

As the class went on I kept a close eye on Kevin. He couldn't stop staring at Brian—his walker, his tiny curled up arms, braced legs. The more I watched, the more I saw. Kevin ran his fingers slowly along the edge of Brian's metal walker, stared curious at its wheels. He was a blind man trying to read with his fingertips, all while I tried to teach the class how to find the Mediterranean Sea on their blackline maps.

It took me the entire class time to figure it out. Kevin had learning issues of his own. He wasn't being a jerk; he was uncomfortable, scared. He saw a child he didn't know with needs he didn't understand and it was all very confusing and scary to him. In the only way he knew how, Kevin was handing me his fears in that situation. And I told him to sit down and be nice. Ugh.

After class I made contact with each of their moms and apologized for both the sum and parts of the situation. I felt terrible and clueless. I could have handled that much better. But the lessons I learned from that situation are invaluable.

Community is messy. You will hurt and be hurt. You will misunderstand and be misunderstood. You won't always say the right thing or do the right thing just as others won't say or do the right thing back. But the critical thing to remember is that it is not failure; it is real life together. The beauty of community is directly dependent on how you navigate the bumps and bruises it produces. Do you see that? Don't be surprised when things get hard and people get hurt, be ready to roll up your sleeves and practice the real work of confession and reconciliation—the gospel lived out in real time. These aren't biblical practices to be ignored, these are life practices to be learned and lived out here, now, in real community.

In His own words Jesus commanded us to love others as He loves us, and then He defined exactly what that looks like: "Greater love has no one than this, than to lay down one's life for his friends" (John 15:13). Jesus was giving us both the model and the guide. The command and the ultimate expression of living that out. Love as I have loved, with complete selflessness.

Paul called that kind of love out in the church of Ephesus as well. In chapter 5 when encouraging the Ephesians to live carefully and wisely, he told them to submit to one another in the fear of Christ (v. 21). Do you see how this is coming full circle? *Love others as I have loved you—fully, lavishly, selflessly, humbly—and then submit to them, lay down your life for them in fear, full awareness, awe, and submission to who you know I am. I* AM.

This is it, friend. This is the missing link to doing community well. Because honestly none of us are nice enough, kind enough, or forgiving enough on our own. We are ungracious and selfish and misunderstanding. We tell people to sit down and shut up in a hundred different graceful and passive-aggressive ways. We misunderstand their fear and confusion and step on them instead. The only grace we have to offer is the grace of Jesus Christ crucified, that crazy love imparted to us so that we may in turn do our best to extend it to others. He modeled it and by His Spirit He empowers it, that He may overflow in us and through us to others as we fear Him.

This is good news. For our salvation and for our communities. We can do life messy together and practice extending grace together as well. And in that devotion and dedication, in that loyalty and commitment we receive the gracious benefits of a full body functioning together. Hands and feet, all members— different and yet growing and learning from one another. Kevin learning from Brian, and me learning from Kevin. Family and friends, in-laws and out-laws and co-workers learning to talk out hard things and seek understanding and trust the good in each other's hearts and in each other's kids. Confession and forgiveness, reconciliation and faith. Grace is so good and beautiful.

This is community that is hard and lovely, edifying and ultimately glorifying Christ. It is in this vein that we get to speak like the psalmist: "Come and hear, all you who fear God and I will declare what He has done for my soul" (Psalm 66:16). We will grow and share and keep telling of how He is using and changing us, together. And as we do, we live our story bravely, one that speaks profoundly of Him. We are laying the foundation of a godly heritage, lived out in community, for our children and the world around us to see.

I wish I would have known more, understood more, about the richness of community while I grieved the loss of Alison. My reflex to protect and hunker down was strong and stubborn and I'm certain I missed out on rich connection and growth, depth of relationship in community because of my lack of vulnerability in that season. Have you been there, pushing away the very gift your heart needs because you are too scared, too protective, to see it as such?

God's redemption is sweet. He has grown and is growing me here. Through unexpected lessons with sweet students and friends who have chosen to push past protective defensiveness and minister to a hundred different hurts, I have seen the beauty of community on display in magnificent ways. And I want more of it. I need more of it. You do too.

Don't fear the messiness of community. We learn to fear God through it. We learn to know Him and trust Him and let the truth of who He is change us, sanctify us, as we grow in grace with others. That is choosing brave. Diving into messy community is choosing brave.

Enjoy the beauty of life with others—camaraderie and encouragement and doing dishes until midnight. Appreciate the hard and new moments, the missteps and misunderstandings, because His grace keeps growing there as well. And you will be able to declare as David did:

> Oh how great is Your goodness, which You have laid up for those who fear you, which You have prepared for those who trust in you in the presence of the sons of men. (Psalm 31:19)

CHAPTER 16

Give Me Grace

Twas grace that taught my heart to fear and grace my fears relieved. How precious did that grace appear the hour I first believed.

John Newton, "Amazing Grace"

Is there a more beautiful word than *grace*? *Charis* in the Greek. Vine's defines it as pleasure, delight, divine favor.[1] It charms and leaves us changed, slighting what we deserve and leaving the good we don't in its stead. You might glimpse it in the every day—a gift of reprieve, an unusually helpful child, kind words from a friend. Grace.

It's the sunset or scenery that gives you pause, a groaning and expectant creation offering quiet delight. It's a friendship or marriage hurt so badly and yet healed so fully, even the scars are hard to recognize. Grace. At its fullest, most incomprehensible, it's Christ's life for ours, at our very worst. It's perfection ripped apart, torn and bled out on our behalf to in turn offer us eternity with Him. Grace.

How could we not be attracted to this? Not want to run headlong into it? It was a slice of that favor I glimpsed fifteen months later, when two pink lines appeared on the stick. I was pregnant again. Grace.

There was no medical reason to believe I wouldn't arrive there. I had one healthy boy, now two and a half years old, before I delivered Alison to heaven. The conclusion was that my loss was rare. "Don't give up. Try again," the doctor had advised with the simplicity of a carnie operating games on the midway. Her casual tone simultaneously calmed my fears and made me wonder if she really understood the nightmare I had just lived. *Try again?*

In time, however, we would, although we may have had more success on those rigged carnival games. At least then we would have an ugly pink lion or maybe a cheap rainbow unicorn to show for our efforts. I, the girl who got pregnant on demand the first time around and by surprise the second time, was now the girl charting cycles and crying fresh tears every twenty-eight days. I wondered if this would be my whole story. Did I just need to settle in here?

A positive test finally came and, with it, more tears. If God bottles tears like David says in Psalm 56, He must have had some really big bottles, a whole storage section, for this season of my life. There is profound gratitude, a tree of life,[2] Proverbs tells us, in the fulfillment of hope deferred. Considering my past, my doubts, and the wait we had now endured, the truth of life growing inside of me again felt like pure grace.

About twenty gloriously uneventful weeks later, we would learn this little life was a baby girl. Grace. And she would be born two years, nearly to the day, after Alison was born. Grace.

This is the grace we like to speak of, the stories we like to tell on repeat. This is the grace we like to hear sermons of. The undeserved gift is beautiful, attractive. We are awed by it, as we should be, but we do grace a disservice when our minds only park there. Getting what we *don't deserve* is only truly amazing when we understand what we *do deserve*.

Acknowledging What We Deserve

High-risk pregnancy has taught me the masterpiece of every life created. Deon, my dear friend who survived the untenable pain of burying her eleven-month-old son, Rion, who never fully recovered from his premature birth, told me once how she finds it interesting that we call babies "miracles" when they fight through birth defects or severe challenges. We've all heard it, right? Those are the *miracle babies*. But the real miracle, Deon says, are the babies who are born without any complications at all. Think about that. Her words pay tribute to the vast number of cells and systems that must be formed and functioning, all working in sync and symmetry, in order for a baby to enter the world free of complications. Birth, life, health truly *is* a miracle. And we just call that normal.

I never understood that with my firstborn. How could I have? My ignorance is a little embarrassing now, but I unknowingly *expected* life, ease, perfection. I didn't fully appreciate the miracle of healthy life growing inside of me until I lived the painful fragility of that. Understanding the miracle of life shifted my gaze from the outcome to the Source.

A.W. Tozer warns the church of the very same ignorance in his study on the fear of God: "The effort of liberal and borderline modernists to woo men to God by presenting the soft side of religion is an unqualified evil because it ignores the very reason for our alienation from God in the first place."[3] Do you see what he's saying? We are not capable of fully understanding the grace of God until we fully understand who He is and our separation from Him. We can't begin to comprehend what it means to get what we don't deserve if we don't first acknowledge what we do deserve: "For all have sinned and fall short of the glory of God" (Romans 3:23).

His glory, His grace is not earned or deserved. Ever. But in His holy greatness He came and dwelt among us, full of grace and truth. And of His fullness we have all received grace upon grace. While we were still sinners, knee-deep in our gory mess of self and disobedience, eyeing every sort of glory but His, He gave His life for us.

This is who He is, friend. We *must* park here—grasp the depths of what we have been saved from—to know what that saving grace even begins to mean.

John Newton got it. After spending many years whiling about, fighting the results of his own poor choices and equally difficult circumstances he did not choose, John Newton found Christ at the age of twenty-three. He wrote of his conversion in his famous hymn, "Amazing Grace": "'Twas grace that taught my heart to fear, and grace my fears relieved."

The familiarity of this hymn might cause us to sing that line like we sing the alphabet, but the weight of those lyrics is profound. Newton understood that it was the grace of God that taught him the fear of God, and that same grace, that same gift and security, that relieved his fear of everything else. This is grace exchanging horizontal fear for vertical fear, rightly aligned fear.

We cheapen the grace of God when we fail to acknowledge who He is and the price He paid to offer that grace. To fully understand the goodness of what we are saved for, we must understand what we are saved from and the great price paid by our Savior. The restoration of relationship with Him for eternity is the prize, but only because of who He is first. We like to run hard to grace, as well we should; it should shatter us. But it only does when we recognize and understand the cost, the propensity, and the depth of love of One holy, righteous, and just. We are saved by His grace, thank God. But can we understand what that means if we never venture to ask what we are saved from?

In Tozer's words, "No one can know the true grace of God who has not first known the fear of God."[4]

What we're talking about here is the gift shifting our focus to the Giver. We work to train our kids in this, right? At every birthday party up until they are about eight years old, we give the same command after each opened gift: "Bailey, what do you say? What do you tell Grandma and Grandpa?" Are we actually increasing their gratitude with our reminders? Of course not, but we're trying to train their gaze. Yes, that gift is good. Yes, gratitude is important, but even more we are teaching our kids to make a connection. Without the giver, there is no gift.

When my oldest son, Tyler, turned four more than a decade ago, he was really into Thomas the Train. He collected the little trains, knew them all by name and set up tracks around our home on a daily basis. For his birthday he wanted nothing more than Cranky the Crane, a cute railway crane with a hook that raised and lowered to move freight amongst the train cars. When I say he wanted this crane for his birthday, understand that he *really*, with all of his four-year-old self, wanted this crane. It was all he asked for, repeatedly. And of course a grandparent obliged and the fifteen-dollar crane was the first gift he opened as we celebrated him over dinner one evening.

Thrilled at the fulfillment of his desire, Tyler was fixated on his gift. I followed the typical parenting script, urging him to thank his grandparents for their kindness, but he barely took his eyes off the crane and mumbled a weakly audible thank-you. He desperately wanted to run to his bedroom and set up his trains and tracks, but I denied his pleading as there were guests waiting and more gifts to open. But he wasn't interested. As hard as I tried, I could not get that kid interested in more gifts or more people or more thank-yous. He didn't care about the other gifts or any of the gifters. He was fixated on one gift.

We aren't four-year-olds stuck in our selfish reflexes. Well, maybe some days. But in maturity we see beyond the gift to the Giver. We see the psalmist do the same thing in Psalm 130:1–4:

> Out of the depths I cry to you, O LORD! O Lord, hear my voice! Let your ears be attentive to the voice of my pleas for mercy! If you, O LORD, should mark iniquities, O Lord, who could stand? But with you there is forgiveness, that you may be feared. (ESV)

Do you see how the psalmist processes the grace of forgiveness? He sees the reasoning, the impetus, that the holy One who forgives may be feared. I don't want to make this out to be an either/or proposition. Don't get me wrong; we need grace every bit as much as we need to fear the Lord. This is both/and. But we must fight hard against the tendency to trade one for the other, prioritize or popularize one over the other. Historically we have done that. The hellfire and wrath of God sermons that trended in the 1700s have fallen out of circulation in favor of the grace and prosperity gospel.

We're beginning to see the backlash of this trend as you don't have to sit long in church circles to hear warnings or snide comments about the prosperity gospel. We've got our guards up against this flagrant teaching and could name a few of those prosperity preachers with ease. We can name them and shame them, but do we seek to right the ship back to center?

We don't need to make the Scripture popular, friend; we need only to see it for what it is. Yes, He is grace. Yes, we are to fear Him. What if we jumped off the pendulum of popular thought and cracked open our Bibles to see Him for who He is, so ridiculously far beyond our trends? He is timeless and unchanging. We don't need to focus on a particular attribute of Him to make Him more palatable for the populous. The very thought of that is embarrassing and sounds faintly reminiscent of the Israelites fashioning Him in the image of a golden calf. It's completely absurd and yet beginning to look familiar.

In the opening chapter of 1 Peter, the apostle tells us to get ready, prepare our minds for action, and set our hope on the grace that will be brought when Christ comes again.[5] He reminds us of God's call in Leviticus to "be holy, for I am holy,"[6] and to conduct ourselves with fear as we live our time here. This is our calling, friend. In and amid the hard and disappointing, intermingled with the overwhelming good and beautiful, our role is the same. Be ready. Set your mind on grace. And pursue holiness through the fear of the Lord. Never either/or, always both/and. Let's get to it.

CHAPTER 17

Necessity

The first step in solving a problem is to recognize it does exist.

Zig Ziglar

Watching people in crisis is always fascinating. Everyone responds so differently to the unsettling shocks of life. Some people get angry, some get quiet and melt. Some become obsessive and others spring into action like agile felines, adapting easily with an innate sense of what to do.

While I sometimes like to pretend I am an agile feline, I'm not. In moments of shock I find it hard to prioritize and categorize. On an average day I can queue incoming data with relative ease. The crying child should likely be addressed now; bills can be addressed later. Dinner must be addressed now and the deadline must be addressed now; laundry will be addressed later. This is how we manage busy lives, a myriad of needs and issues flying at us. We rank, sort, and file with skill. Most of the time, anyhow.

But occasionally, unexpectedly, a piece of our earth quakes. Then it all seems important and incredibly unimportant at the very same time. Fragile. My sense of prioritization vaporizes and I only then notice what a vital skill it is, was. I get foggy, confused, and overwhelmed. Have you been there?

On the podcast Knowing Faith, I recently heard a discussion about spiritual triage. Maybe it's because I work in a medical office that the concept instantly resonated with me, but if you've ever been to a hospital or doctor's office, it will likely make sense to you as well. Triage is the winnowing fork of the medical community—where they quickly size up a patient's situation, evaluate the medical attention needed, and prioritize how long you will be waiting. Roughly 99 percent of people who walk through the door of an ER or doctor's office believe their need is important. Very important. Triage is a quick way for medical professionals to determine what is truly a first-degree issue and help those with the greatest need first.

When we look at the whole of Scripture or the whole of good and faithful teachers speaking out on biblical concepts, we can easily feel like a waiting-room patient. Isn't *everything* important?

Outline biblical wisdom and instruction on a tidy to-do list and you will quickly be overcome by the weight of it all. We need to serve our families and lead our children. We need to love our husbands well and model and teach that to the women walking behind us. We must discover and develop our spiritual gifts, continue gutting our own sin issues, care for the widow and orphan, love our neighbors far and near, honor and respect authority, pursue wisdom and humility, all while doing the daily work of keeping our homes managed, bills paid, and our people fed. Are you tired yet? Confused yet? Weary yet?

I don't for a second want to contradict the good work we are called to do. Stay with me here and we'll learn that there is no contradiction or competition among them, but sometimes a bit of spiritual triage is helpful. We are commanded, in no uncertain terms, to love the Lord our God see with *all* of our heart and soul and mind and strength (Luke 10:27). Did you catch that? Basically the whole operating system *and* the grit. Everything. All in, loving Him. God gives us this commandment through Moses in Deuteronomy and reiterates it in the Gospels. We are instructed to use everything we possess, everything that's in us to love Him. That's a high calling, friend.

Scripture also gives an equally weighty priority to fearing the Lord. Remember in Proverbs 9:10 we are told that "the fear of the LORD is the *beginning* of wisdom, and knowledge of the Holy One is understanding."[1] And in Proverbs 1:7, "The fear of the LORD is the beginning of knowledge, but fools despise wisdom and instruction." If we are doing triage, the Word is making it fairly clear. You want wisdom and knowledge? You want direction and guidance, discernment and understanding? Start here. Godly fear *precedes* wisdom and knowledge. Or as Job said, "The fear of the Lord—that is wisdom."[2]

We are instructed to love Him fully and fear Him. And from that heart posture proceeds knowledge, wisdom, and understanding. From that place we learn hope and humility, we are given a heritage and even a friendship with the Lord (see Psalm 25:14). And the most fascinating part is how these terms are all interrelated and connected. When we begin not just to know *of Him* but really *know* Him, we love and fear Him. When we love and fear Him, we seek to know Him more. This is the abundance and fullness of God: More of Him always equals more of Him. And more of Him will always mean more identity-deep courage, bravery to walk confidently in our everyday lives.

Can we have, say, humility without fearing God? Absolutely, a humility that points right back to us. If that sounds like an idiosyncrasy, it should. Can we have a heritage without fearing the Lord? Absolutely a heritage without God, a heritage of self-efficacy, that plants a flourishing orchard of tainted apples for the next generation to feast on. Without a complete love for and fear of the Lord, we cannot expect anything good to come from our lives, but with it, good fruit becomes the natural by-product.

This cures our appetite for works-based righteousness, cuts it off at the quick. Catch a wide-eyed glimpse at how massive our God is and that little deed you're trying to pull off, maybe impress Him with just a little, looks pretty paltry by comparison. Grasp a pinhole of His greatness, His righteousness, His purity, from the sin-drenched dregs of your own heart and it's game over. Filthy rags.

And still He loves. Still He chose the cross for us. Still He chooses to do beautiful ministry in and through us. And so we work, not out of obligation or servitude, but out of honor and love. A full circle offering back to Him. Scripture sings this message in ways we so often glance right past:

As the heavens are high above the earth, so great is His mercy toward those who fear Him. (Psalm 103:11)

The mercy of the LORD is from everlasting to everlasting on those who fear Him, and His righteousness to children's children. (Psalm 103:17)

Better is a little with the fear of the LORD, than great treasure with trouble. (Proverbs 15:16)

The fear of the LORD is the instruction of wisdom, and before honor is humility. (Proverbs 15:33)

The fear of the Lord is not an add-on. It isn't sprinkles on top or the latest allergen we've all successfully managed to eradicate from our diet for better digestion. *I'm FF, fear-of-the-Lord free.* We can't toss Scripture, our light and lamp, like we do unhealthy or unpopular ingredients. It's not a dietary plan; *it is life.* The Word is not subject to trends or even our limited understanding. Just because words have fallen out of favor in our culture does not excuse us from the truth they mandate. Let that settle for a minute. Trends do not change Truth.

Good Growth

I live in ag country, just outside the city limits. Our home is hemmed in by crops on every side. And believe it or not, trends are quite a thing here. I never much realized it before we moved to the country, but the fertile soil and temperate climate we live in makes for excellent growing conditions for a wide variety of agriculture. Blueberries and plums, apricots and apples, corn, hay, hops, and grapes of all varieties—we grow them here. And they cycle.

Hops were a dying crop a few years back. Fields, barren and empty, were converted to something more profitable, only to make a comeback as craft breweries have risen in popularity. Hop fields now pepper the landscape as the crop is once again profitable.

Tastes and trends impact our economy here. They affect the workforce, the equipment and machinery businesses, the seed and spray companies. They affect the view from my window. But they do not change the truth underlying farming. Farmers need to make a living. In order to survive, they need to pay their expenses and turn a profit on what they grow. Peaches or cherries or triticale—the crops have to cash flow in order for the farmer to continue producing them. That is the truth of the industry and the weight with which farmers mete out challenges to growing certain crops. They do triage.

Rising water costs might not be a huge deal. Water rationing is. Higher seed prices may not have a big impact, while lower market prices can move the needle quickly. Do you see how farming triage might occur? Challenges must be seen, noticed, weighed.

The same could be said of us as believers. There are trends in our churches, both locally and globally. We may lean toward traditional hymns or newer songs of worship and back again. We may prefer the New King James version of the Bible or a smoother, modern translation, but we must understand the impact of our trade-offs. We must do triage and in the push of changing tides, realize what is up for negotiation and what is simply not.

This is what comes to my mind when I hear someone say the fear of the Lord is outdated or old terminology. It's definitely a bit dusty, something we have knowingly or unknowingly relegated to the back burner. But when we unpack both the relevance and prevalence of it in Scripture, we should quickly realize the error in our neglect here. The fear of the Lord is a nonnegotiable:

Fear the Lord, you his holy people, for those who fear him lack nothing. The lions may grow weak and hungry, but those who seek the Lord lack no good thing. Come, my children, listen to me; I will teach you the fear of the Lord. (Psalm 34:9–11 niv)

The Lord of hosts, him you shall honor as holy. Let him be your fear, and let him be your dread. (Isaiah 8:13 esv)

Honor everyone. Love the brotherhood. Fear God. Honor the emperor. (1 Peter 2:17 esv)

I could keep on listing, keep on dusting off the Scripture we've been breezing by for years, but I want to leave plenty for you. Watch as you read the Word and study. It's like when you were first pregnant or even just hoping to be. You start seeing pregnant women *everywhere*. Our gaze turns and with it, our hearts. *God, let it be so.*

We've heard for years that God commands us to be strong and courageous, to not fear. And it is true, friend. But how about we start paying attention to what, or rather whom, He tells us *to fear*. New Testament or Old, let's be watching. This is not irrelevant or impertinent. It's ancillary, necessary. It's the proper way we relate to our God, the King of kings. Both intimate and expansive, big and close. Grace and truth. Never opposites, but rather all-encompassing.

The fruit He bestows on those who honor Him is a most beautiful gift, but never more beautiful than the Giver. May we continue to seek Him, know Him, and learn to fear Him as we follow Him.

CHAPTER 18

Intimacy

At the heart of the Christian message is God Himself waiting for His redeemed children to push in to conscious awareness of His Presence.

A.W. Tozer

The lyrics of Steffany Gretzinger and Amanda Cook's song, "Out of Hiding," gave me pause the first time I heard them. You know how that is, when music is just background noise, but some of the words creep past your ears and settle someplace deeper. The simple tune of this song is paired with pure and weighty lyrics that speak of God's call for us to come close, to forsake hiding—attempting to cover our ugly past and present failures—covering all that He already knows, sees, *loves*. One line in particular kept turning over and over again in my head, *"No need to be frightened of intimacy."*

Is that it? The chasm between so many of us and God seems vast. I meet woman after woman who knows Him, who is a regular in the Sunday morning pew, and yet there is a distance between her and God that she has become comfortable with. For many years, I have been her. Is it because we are scared, frightened to come close?

I have brought up this question in conversation with friends and in conversation with God. *Are we frightened to know you, Lord? Have I been scared to draw near fully, deeply?*

My mind flashes back to Moses, shoes off, trembling at the burning bush. Joshua facedown before the Commander of the Lord's army. Distance dissolved.

The bleeding woman knew it. Her fear of man vanished in Christ's dusty footprints as she set her eyes on her Savior. She came poor and empty, the life literally draining out of her for years. And she came close. Thick among the crowds, she wedged nearer, reached and grabbed hold of what she could of Jesus. The hem of His robe would be sufficient. And it was. Don't you love that visual?

When Jesus Christ chose to be the ultimate sacrifice for our sin, the veil was torn. The separation that *was necessary* has been obliterated. He left a Helper in His stead, and for you and me that means God is big and He is close. Yes, we are called to fear Him, we have established that fact, but on the other side of that fear, through it, we are invited to intimacy and nearness like never before. Let's follow that bleeding woman a little longer:

> When the woman saw that she had not escaped notice, she came trembling and fell down before Him, and declared in the presence of all the people the reason why she had touched Him, and how she had been immediately healed. (Luke 8:47 NASB)

She is now the non-bleeding, used-to-be-bleeding woman, but in that same moment she is exposed, seen. She had more courage to forsake the law, to come out of hiding when she believed she could escape notice, blend in. But when Jesus feels power leave His body and calls out, "Who touched me?" I can only imagine the earthquake that erupts inside of her.

Luke says she came trembling and fell down; Mark says she came in fear and trembling. But she didn't whisper, whimper, while the eyes of the crowd turned toward her. Can you envision the mass disdain? Even so she declared for all the wild world to see. She declared.

She told Jesus the whole truth of how she was immediately healed. And He looked on her with compassion. Called her daughter. Commended her faith. And granted her peace. What a picture of godly fear and holy courage. What a picture of our God—a King whom we are to fear, but not at arm's length, held at a distance. A King who desires us to draw near, nearer still, toward the intimacy of a Father.

Stepping Near

I was that bleeding woman. Maybe you were, *are*, too? The details of our stories vary. But the truth of who He is amid our disappointment, our ache, our lack, and our years of trying, our poor and empty, do not. Often we take the details of our present situation and get comfortable with them rather than confront them.

Pay attention to the way you talk about fear—the way you speak of it, the way your husband or friends or kids talk of it—and it's telling. There are things you will gladly admit you're afraid of. Maybe it's spiders or sharks or messing up your kids. These are somewhat acceptable fears, common concerns.

But there are a whole host of things we won't admit to being frightened of. "I'm not scared to start a business, to lead a Bible study, to mentor someone else. I'm just not sure it's the right time." We often offer up flimsy excuses for our fears and those paper-thin excuses are so common and comfortable, we readily accept and receive them rather than call them out for what they are in our friends and in ourselves.

Am I frightened to know you, God? Am I scared of becoming weird, to go all in, of losing my autonomy or independence? Am I holding back? Am I ashamed of my too-ugly past and real-messy present? Does obedience frighten me and comparison horrify me? Am I embarrassed by how much I don't know and flat scared of disappointing you, of failing you? God, am I scared of knowing you?

In our isolation, the quiet recesses of our minds, these questions, fears, feel original and too much. And yet when we peek back into Genesis, we find that they are age-old and quite familiar.

> They heard the sound of the LORD God walking in the garden in the cool of the day, and the man and his wife hid themselves from the presence of the LORD God among the trees of the garden. Then the LORD God called to the man, and said to him, "Where are you?" He said, "I heard the sound of You in the garden, and I was afraid because I was naked; so I hid myself" (Genesis 3:8–10 NASB).

Let's absorb that passage. Adam and Eve had experienced perfect intimacy with God up until this moment. They were free to enjoy Him, delight in Him without self-consciousness or doubt of any kind. They were fully bare, naked, and without shame. We've been clothed and covered for so long it's hard to even imagine, isn't it?

But in their questioning of God, in giving way to the deceit of the serpent and the charm of wisdom apart from God,

Adam and Eve chose sin over God, separation over intimacy, and shame instantly rained down on them. They were wildly aware of their inadequacy, a severance that didn't even exist only a moment ago. Intimacy was dissolved. And they shrank back. They cowered. They hid.

What a heartbreaking shift. Perfect communion was now cloudy with angst and awkwardness, the separation was palpable. Trust on both ends was broken. And from that moment, all of humanity, as Paul Tripp says, "lives in this weird and uncomfortable battle between hunger for God and a desire to hide from him."[1] This is the answer to every one of my fear-tainted questions about intimacy with God, every one of my paper-thin excuses I've offered, believed, for years.

Separation creates an unhealthy fear of God, it widens the gap. While intimacy turns that fear on its head, it bids us to come near in proper fear, submission, and honor, to come close and know Him here. Remember, the fear of the Lord, as we saw it in Moses and Joshua, is a fear that always bids us to come, a fear that thrives in nearness.

In Jeremiah, the prophetic book of separation and judgment, I love how God speaks about the return and reconciliation of His people:

> They shall be my people, and I will be their God; then I will give them one heart and one way, that they may fear me forever, for the good of them and their children after them. And I will make an everlasting covenant with them, that I will not turn away from doing them good; but I will put my fear in their hearts so that will not depart from me. (Jeremiah 32:38–40)

Do you see the fullness of this verse in light of all we have been learning? The beauty of the strength and *courage* that comes from the safety and security of fearing Him? The unique nearness of our relationship with Christ, intimacy bought only by His chosen sacrifice on the cross, offers us all of this. Goodness, nearness, unity, one heart, one way, and a promise of a heritage for our children as well. I hope you see the freedom here, friend. I hope you see the weight of shame broken to pieces, shattered by the weight of His glory, righteousness, and chosen nearness.

His broken body has afforded our brave. His passionate and sacrificial desire to draw us near, to see Him and know Him and rightly fear Him changes everything. Why would we ever hide from that, distance that? The veil was torn and our separation was finished, and now we must summon the courage to leave behind the shame He has already erased and choose to enter in, close, near to the One who destroyed fear of anything else but His own pure and righteous holiness. May this greatness never be lost on us, may we live aware of it, see it, in ways both large and small.

The other night I did.

I am the very definition of early to bed, early to rise. It's my life on repeat. So when my six-year-old son, Bo, approached my bed just minutes after 10 p.m., the haze of sleepiness had already paralyzed my brain.

"Mom, am I going to have to go to the doctor?" His normally cheery voice was weak, almost trembling, shrouded in fear even a sleepy mom could notice.

"Uh, no. I don't know. What's wrong?" I willed my brain to engage like peddling a bike uphill. He offered no words and instead, evidence. He lifted his little hand to show me a cymbal attached to his index finger. If this makes no sense to your fully awake brain, you can imagine how I processed this with my sluggish one.

"Is there a . . . cymbal attached to your . . . finger?" Bo nodded slowly, eyes wide. I am an engager by nature, a determined fix-it girl, and as my mind made as much sense of this as it possibly could, I slipped into that natural role like familiar bed slippers. I took a closer look at the cymbal, which was once part of his Christmas drum set. (One word: *grandparents.*) Apparently he had removed the top hat cymbal and tried it on as the most awkward ring ever. The cymbal fit there perfectly, and that chubby base of his tiny index finger seemed to hold it in place like a Chinese finger lock. It wasn't budging.

"Okay, this is no big deal, buddy," I told him. "Once, when I was a little girl, I got a ring stuck on my finger and my mom just rubbed it with a little lotion and it came right off." I led him to my bathroom and awkwardly applied lotion around all contact points of his tiny finger and this big, gawky cymbal-ring. And it did not budge a bit.

My expertise and ingenuity fully expended, I led my boy downstairs to where Ross and Tyler were watching a late movie together. "Babe, I need help."

You should know Ross is more business and a little less cheery-voice than I am. It's a good balance. As he caught sight of the problem, he gave me a somewhat discreet *What in the world?* look and tugged gently at the cymbal. Still stuck.

"Let me grab something, buddy" were his only words as he left the room.

Ross is an electrician. He has lots of tools, and he came back quickly with a pair of cutters he calls dikes—a hand tool with heavy blades that looked like they could easily snip Bo's entire finger off quite neatly. They are what he uses to cut through thick wire on a regular basis.

Ross gave Bo a serious stare. "I need you to hold very still, buddy. This won't hurt, but you have to be still." The tiniest tear escaped Bo's eyelid and his lips trembled as he forced the fear to stay put, to trust the dad whom he knew loved him. Ross made multiple, careful cuts into the cymbal, dismantling it in distorted pieces and ultimately freeing Bo's finger in just a minute or two. In his freedom, Bo turned and wept. He curled himself into my neck as far as he could. He was safe.

Bo's my baby, so you can imagine how I soaked that moment up. But it spoke of something greater to me. It spoke of real fear and perceived fear. Healthy fear and unhealthy fear. It spoke of real safety and perceived safety. It spoke of trembling in the face of something greater than us and trembling in the face of a fear that is our safety, our freedom. It spoke of the intimacy, compassion, and care of a father. It spoke of courage, not of our own, not in our own ability, but in one who knows more, loves more, than we can ever imagine. This moment spoke of letting faith in that knowledge be our strength and in its wake, being overcome by our safety. The cleft of the rock.

I wish my little guy didn't have to walk through that terrifying moment, but I'm grateful for the lesson—for both him and *us*. And as I look back on it, I wonder: How long did it take Bo to come to us? Did he stay in his room, hidden for a few minutes? Did he hesitate to show us what he had done? It was hours past his bedtime—was he sitting in his room, tugging at that cymbal, scared the entire time? Was he hiding, ashamed, frightened of all the wrong things instead of just coming to us, drawing near, humbly?

I doubt I'll ever know the answers to those questions, but perhaps they can serve us well. What have we allowed between us and Christ? How have we hidden from Him? In what ways have we used distance as a form of protection, convinced ourselves our problems are too small or unworthy of His attention?

Waiting, sitting long with that stuck cymbal, is a travesty of lost time and missed grace. God bids us to come near. We were designed for intimacy with Him so that we might bear His image and glory to the world around us as sons and daughters. No hiding.

CHAPTER 19

Freedom

*For freedom Christ has set us free; stand firm therefore, and
do not submit again to a yoke of slavery.*

Apostle Paul

Oddly enough, in the aftermath of delivering Alison, one of
the things I feared most was my new identity. I was a bereaved
mother. The mother of a stillborn. I have always hated everything about that word, *stillborn*. Now that was *my* word. It felt
attached, an appendage. This is me.

I hated the sad-eyed stares from well-meaning acquaintances
I bumped into while running errands. I knew their intentions
were wholly good, as were mine when I had offered that same
sympathetic gaze in the past. But remember, I'm a little do-it-
yourself by nature and I wanted *so badly* to turn off that faucet
of reflexive pity, both for them and me. *Can you please just go
on? Can I please look someone in the eye without apologies,*

a subtle sigh, or slight left turn of the chin? Can I just be a normal person again?

Maybe the questions I felt, the fears that fueled them, had less to do with "can I," but will I?

Apparently I wasn't the first one to wonder how to move forward once what feels sacred, close, foundational, is no more. David asked the same question: "When the foundations are destroyed, what can the righteous do?" (Psalm 11:3 CSB).

Sometimes these new identities slip themselves on us, sometimes we choose them. At times they come as a result of our decisions, other times they are thrust upon us by the decisions of others. And *every time* they are ill-fitting—who we think we are, who someone else says we are—yet none of it feels natural or comfortable or true.

We might step into that new identity for lack of a better option or maybe not even realizing we had an option. We click the leaden overalls securely atop each shoulder, adjust the straps in search of a better fit. This is it, right? This is who I am now. The girl who had a stillborn baby. Or maybe, the alcoholic, the addict. The mother of a prodigal. The woman without breasts. Bereft of any other option, we bootstrap those identities into new and hard places. We absorb them until they pulse free in our bloodstream. *This is who I am now.*

But when we do that, overnight or over years, we deny the blood that streamed for us. When we chose Christ, who first chose us, our identity was forever changed, we are clothed in righteousness. There is no need to keep strapping on overalls of our poor choices, of our unfair circumstances. We are a new creation, identity sure and steady, unchanged and unchanging. Why would we not live free in that?

David steps right up and answers his own question in the very next verse:

The LORD is in his holy temple; the LORD —his throne is in heaven. His eyes watch; his gaze examines everyone. (Psalm 11:4 CSB)

He recognizes that God is on the throne. His eye is on us. Foundations quaking or not, if truth is really true, then it must be true *for us*. *In us*. Backstory, hard past, or hard present notwithstanding.

Can't you see the same Jesus you know throughout Scripture looking you straight in the eye as He did the paralytic? "Stand up," He told him. "Go."[1] Or the woman overcome by her sin in His presence and drowning His feet with her tears? "Your sins have been forgiven," He told her.[2]

To stand on this side, in the fear of God, is the wildest and purest form of courage because you *know* the God who goes before, hems you in from every side. He is wild and untamed. As C.S. Lewis reminds us in *The Lion, the Witch and the Wardrobe*, "He isn't safe. But he's good."[3] You are learning how He loves, how He protects, how He fights battles, and how He is always ultimately victorious. You are trading your eyes for His view. If that does not give you steeled freedom and raw courage, check your pulse, girl, nothing will. This is Him. This is who you are because of who He is and what He has done. It's about time you walk that out. It's about time you lived it.

Just typing those words gets my heart pumping faster, but faster beating hearts are worthless unless we can figure out how to put them into action. How to turn those beats into footsteps and spoken words, art we actually live, and love we actually give because it was freely given first to us. The freedom the fear of the Lord affords leads us to the brink of this. And now we must muster the courage to step.

Stepping Near

I still remember the first time I ever led a meeting. I was the coordinator of a new MOPS group, and the leadership team was gathering to plan and discuss. And I was in charge. My heart was racing and I felt sweaty as I wrote out an agenda. I had never been "in charge" of any formal group of adults before, and the thought of being responsible for the direction, tempo, and pace of this meeting, all of those eyes looking at me for how this was going to go down, scared me. And then I thought of one of my closest friends, Alesha, owner of one set of those eyes that would be staring back at me in that meeting. She *knew* me. She had seen me in good moments and ugly ones. She loved me. The thought of her sitting there staring at me was courage. I could make a fool of myself, say something really dumb, and I knew Alesha would still love me.

I hope you have a parent or a sister or spouse, a friend or a mentor who you *know* will still love you even if you fall on your face. Fall-on-your-face love is empowering. Even now at speaking engagements, I love having a close friend in the audience—a tangible expression of real courage. Because we need that. It's pure gold to know, without words, someone is thinking, *"Go on, girl, give it your all. Speak, sing, dance your heart out. Lead with all you got, parent with both feet wet. Be all in. Go pray for that stranger when it makes you all nervous, and become a mentor with no fear of messing it up—not because you are flawless, but because you couldn't possibly be loved any less."*

Do you see the courage that affords? The good news is you don't need an Alesha. Having one is great, don't get me wrong, but you don't need one. If you have committed your life to Christ, He is fully and forever committed to you. He could not love you more and will never love you less.

He is in the audience. He is at the table. He is in the passenger seat of your car, standing at the side of the hospital bed with you, walking down the funeral home corridor with you, holding vigil with you, and holding you in the vigil. When you choose brave, you are not choosing to see something brave in yourself. You are not choosing to find bravery in the courage of your own Alesha. You are choosing to believe that this bravery is found in Christ alone—with whom you stand and who always, unfailingly, stands with you.

Go right on and give it your all and come up short. Parent all in and still mess up. Forget your lines, look like an airhead or an idiot. Be misunderstood as a jerk. Fail trying. Obviously, this is not the goal, but could it happen? Sure it could, but the fear of that—and almost everything else—is gone, obliterated, when we truly know who He is and how He loves. He could not love you more. Living from that truth begins with believing that it's true.

Paul preaches up a storm with his words to the church at Galatia. His words are delivered to Gentiles getting all caught up in the law and works-based righteousness, wearing outcomes like a cloak—or maybe a noose—around their necks. The overalls of this new identity are securely fastened. But Paul is about to blow their minds with his standard boldness: "For freedom, Christ set us free. Stand firm then, and don't submit again to a yoke of slavery" (Galatians 5:1 CSB). He instructs the Galatians that faith working in love is both the form and function for this freedom, "for you were called to be free, brothers and sisters; only don't use this freedom as an opportunity for the flesh, but serve one another through love" (Galatians 5:13 CSB).

I love how these words travel time and space to meet you and me right where we are. We have been *set* free, to *live* free. That's not so hard to understand on paper, but, girl, we live that out something messy.

We don't move from death to death, but from death to life in Christ. No more bondage to ill-fitting identities, you and I are daughters, coheirs with Christ. Paul is telling the church, don't get all tangled up in the distractions of the law. As he wrote to the Corinthians, "Where the Spirit of the Lord is, there is freedom" (2 Corinthians 3:17 CSB). And he is drilling that same truth here, encouraging the church to *walk* in the Spirit,[4] *be led* by the Spirit,[5] and *live* in the Spirit.[6] Because this is where real freedom comes from. Throw off the sin that is so easily tripping you up. Toss the false identity that you have let own you. Lock eyes with Him, and run your race in freedom, friend.

This freedom is what awaits us on the other side of fearing Him.

We often think of prayer as talking to God, but our communication with Him should be just as much, if not more, listening. Think about it, if you had the opportunity to converse with the wisest person in the room, what would benefit you most—all the talking or all the listening? As Christians we like to encourage one another to talk to God, to "pray about it" when we find ourselves in a tough situation. And maybe that is just the lingo we use, but Paul didn't tell the Galatians to pray for freedom, he told them to get busy—to walk and be led and live. I'm not about to minimize prayer here, but those activities seem to involve a whole lot more listening than talking. Prayer was never meant to be one-way communication, but rather a conversation.

Thankfully we serve a God who values relationship, who loves to know and be known. Our communication is two-way, but sometimes we rely only on the output. We make our request known and never listen for the answers. We pray for courage, for opportunity, for vision, for peace, and in the very next second, we make prompt plans as to how *we* are going fix it.

I do this all the time, even though I know better. Thick in the midst of writing this book and attempting to manage the rest of my responsibilities, I began to feel a bit weary, not tired, but weary. You know, when the finish line is still miles away and your running legs become leaden, your breathing shallow. This is not a normal state for me. The feeling was foreign and concerning.

"I think I need a vacation," I told my husband weakly. "I'm feeling weary." Note that I didn't even pray about it at this point. I had prayed for strength to keep going, but who prays for a vacation. Ridiculous, right?

That afternoon we had to pick up our daughter from ballet. Since it was a Saturday and everyone was home, we decided to go as a family, pick her up, and stop by our favorite little ice cream spot for cones. We sat in the shop, hands filled with drippy waffle cones topped with butter pecan, rainbow sherbet, and chocolate chip mint when the kids asked if we could walk to the park. We're country folk, so the park and city streets with sidewalks always feel like a treat to us. From the park the kids begged to show their dad our small-town museum—the one with the Revolutionary War muskets, and 1800s square grand piano, and words from Theodore Roosevelt's 1906 speech from the train depot of our tiny town.

This isn't how we spend our Saturdays. Ever, really. We work on projects on our small acreage. We go to basketball or flag football games. We cart kids around and get the shopping done. The calendar is nearly always full and Saturday is a get-it-done day.

But on this particular Saturday, as we eventually made our way back to our car, without even thinking, I quipped to my husband, "It kind of feels like we are on vacation." And as soon as the words came out I remembered my complaint that very morning about feeling weary.

Friend, God knows what you need even before you ask.[7] Listen. Pay attention. Whether brave looks like pursuing the rest that He graciously puts in front of you or speaking up and inviting in, listen, pay attention to His promptings, to what He places in front of you. More often than not, you will not need to go seeking opportunities to live with courage, to live wildly from the freedom that is already yours, the freedom He purchased for you. He will place them in front of you. Notice them. Give thanks for them.

Fear Him. Walk. Be led. Choose brave. He is closer, far more worthy, than we even know.

Afterword

My story didn't and doesn't end here. There was eventually another baby and another and another. That makes four of them, six of us. God has used this story, this hard, to grow me and teach me in ways I never imagined. And through it all, it is well.

This isn't the end, but another beginning. For you and for me. We have days to live and decisions to make. Choose brave, friend. I pray He will use these words to penetrate the page and sink deep. Embrace holy courage and live fully in godly fear. No minimizing it or rushing past it. We know what real fear is. We know the One worthy of it. And we know it is only in the intimacy of this relationship that we will ever find real courage. A humble courage. A courage that will become our heritage if we bravely choose it. A fruitful life demands this. Let's get to it.

Thank you for walking and dusting with me. I hope you know Him a bit more. I hope you noticed something new about Him here. The living and active Word never ceases to teach and reach and grow us. That's how it works. It doesn't get old. It never will.

My prayer is that you keep right on noticing. Keep reading the Word faithfully, and keep asking Him for wisdom. Listen. Walk.

Don't buy the lines the world sells. They often have a glimmer of truth in them, but they're always just a shade or two off center. Don't conform to that pattern, hold it up to the light of truth, renew your mind so that you may test and approve.

And have courage, dear heart. Choose brave. You're going to need it. But His strength is sufficient. He is a good guide and has provided a faithful Helper, Comforter, for the journey. Let's move on, all in. Not fearless, but in spite of fear—in fear of the One worthy. Fully knowing there is faith, there is freedom, sheer courage on the other side.

I leave you with words from John the Revelator:[1]

Great and awe-inspiring are your works, Lord God, the Almighty; just and true are your ways, King of the nations. Lord, who will not fear and glorify your name? For you alone are holy. All the nations will come and worship before you because your righteous acts have been revealed. . . .
Amen. Even so, come, Lord Jesus!

DISCUSSION
Questions

Since we're walking together, as friends do—sharing stories and stretching muscles—these questions for the walk will be offered along the path. They are posed for both immediate response and slower churning, always lifting our gaze to see what God might have us see, know, and learn.

Chapter 1—The Truth about Fear

1. Have you ever had a completely irrational, maybe even silly, fear? It's interesting to realize how fear, even the more frivolous ones, impacts us in tangible ways. Think about how that fear impacted you. Did your heart race? Did your palms sweat? Did the possibility of it becoming real captivate your thoughts and run wild?

2. Our fears are directional, always pointing toward what we prize. Have you ever considered this? Pause and

think about patterns of fear in your own life. What do these patterns point toward?

3. Proverbs tells us the fear of the Lord is the beginning of both wisdom and knowledge. Don't let the familiarity of those verses slip past you. Read them in Proverbs 1:7 and 9:10. Mark them in your Bible. We know we need wisdom. In fact, we prayed for it together as we started this walk, remember? And now the author is showing us the path. David is essentially saying, "Begin here." What might pursuing wisdom and knowledge look like in your daily life as you consider fearing the Lord?

Chapter 2—What Do I Know of Holy?

1. Defining terms is an important basis for any good discussion. So let's start here. How have you defined the fear of the Lord in the past? How have you defined courage? Do these definitions align with what you know of Scripture?

2. What do you think it means to *choose brave*? Do you think your definition differs from what the culture markets as brave?

3. Where has fear plagued you? Sneaky or obvious, what fears have diseased your confidence, captivated your mind, or been tucked away tidily in your heart? Pause and invite God into that specific place. Invite His Holy Spirit, our Helper, to teach you and to provide greater understanding of who He is in relation to your specific point of pain. He promises wisdom to those who ask; let's have the courage to ask, friend.

Chapter 3—When Life Gets Your Attention

1. In what moments has life expectedly or unexpectedly gotten your attention? How did you initially respond? How do those moments/memories linger?

2. We've talked about Moses and Joshua twice now. Take a minute to read these accounts for yourself in your own Bible. If you've heard these stories since childhood, take a deep breath and try to see them anew, meet them with the maturity of time and experience. Put yourself in their shoes. Or better yet, take them off. You'll find Moses at the burning bush in Exodus 3 and Joshua with the angel of the Lord's army in Joshua 5:13–15. What do these stories say about fearing the Lord? In what ways do they encourage your fear of the Lord?

3. Moses became acutely aware of God's presence in the most casual of coordinates. Why do you think God chose to show up there? Burning bushes aside, how do you think God meets us in our own casual coordinates today?

Chapter 4—Good-Bye Fearlessness

1. Psalm 86:11 says, "Teach me Your way, O LORD; I will walk in Your truth; unite my heart to fear Your name." Ponder that for a minute. Why would David pray for the Lord to unite his heart to fear God? How might our hearts be led astray, split, divided, desperately in need of God to unite them in order to fear Him?

2. Where has fearlessness captivated your gaze and attention? How does the world around you encourage and

celebrate it? What are we neglecting, trading, in our hunger for fearlessness?

3. What would a new script look like for you? If bootstrapping is your tendency, your reflex, and is the advice the world gives, what practical strategies can you come up with for fixing your gaze when the pressure around you mounts?

Chapter 5—Someone Worth Fearing

1. In my instinct to protect and right all that was going wrong, I focused my attention on the tragedy in front of me, inside of me, rather than the God who goes before me. Think back on the challenges of your life. How do you respond when things go wrong? What is reflexive for you?

2. Grab your Bible and underline the pronouns in Exodus 3:7–10. Let those words jump off the page for you. Also reread Moses' response in verse 11. Can you resonate with Moses, stuck fast with your eyes on . . . *you?*

3. While you have your Bible, move over to Psalm 29 and read it. Then flip back a couple pages and read Psalm 34. Do you think we have a tendency to make God smaller than He is? We need these truths committed deeply, planted firmly *now*, so we don't lose sight, lose focus when things get tough.

Chapter 6—Smaller Gods

1. Amid challenges, the temptation to dispel the darkness and alleviate the ache is real. We want to fix it, assuage it, or at least temper it. Have you felt this in your life? In

what areas do you most feel the knee-jerk reaction to fix it?

2. What lesser gods have you become comfortable with? Sit with that a minute. What have you relied upon to distract and comfort you, appease or satisfy you rather than waiting for God? This isn't fun to think about, but our patterns and habits are worth uncovering in the Light.

3. Remember who He is. Train your reflexes. Begin by reading Isaiah 46:8–11 and weigh the truth of who God is against any of the appeasing options you uncovered in the previous question. He is God and there is none like Him.

Chapter 7—On Trend

1. The question the doctor posed to me felt like a serpentine olive branch. What serpentine olive branches have you come across in your own life? What temporary appeasements, compromises that might appear attractive, forbidden apples, have dangled in front of you?

2. Have you noticed trends in Christian culture? Beyond surface styles, have you noticed shifts that seem more foundational? How do those shifts align with the unchanging truth of God and what He has given us in Scripture?

3. Go back to Exodus 3 again. You should be getting comfortable with that spot by now. Read verses 13–14. Why do you think God chose to call himself I am?

Chapter 8—Curiosity and Obedience

1. Do you live curious? Do you look at hills and valleys and unfamiliar paths along the way as opportunities to

lean in to what unexpected, good, sweet, and even hard learning God has planned for you? Do you move toward or away from Him in these moments?

2. Read of Paul's conversion in Acts 9. Notice the acuity of Paul's pivot. It's immediate. He has two questions: "Who are you, Lord?" and "What do you want me to do?" We all need pivots at times. Consumed or distracted by the journey, we lose sight of curiosity and obedience to the One worthy. Maybe it's time to pause and ask Him the very same questions. Journal your prayers, thoughts, questions, and answers from the Word right here. What might be some pivot points you need to make?

3. Read Colossians 3:22 and Ephesians 6:5. How do we do good work here on earth? Our earnest obedience here is dependent upon what?

Chapter 9—Vulnerability

1. Have you seen the theme of vulnerability rise in popularity in recent years? What positive and negative impacts have you noticed, felt, experienced?

2. Vulnerability always feels risky. And it is, in almost every place in our lives besides our relationship with the Lord. This is the safest place for our vulnerability. Let's do a little word study. Now that we've dusted off a good share of Scripture that commands us to fear the Lord, let's unpack the fruit that grows rich in this soil. Take some time to flip through the following verses in the book of Psalms, stacked right up behind and before David's journal entry we just read from Psalm 31. Take some notes on what grows here. Psalm 25:14;

Psalm 31:19; Psalm 34:7; Psalm 61:5; Psalm 85:9; Psalm 103:11, 13; Psalm 115:13; Psalm 145:19; Psalm 147:11. What do you find here? In what ways might you apply those to your life?

3. Take a moment to think through Jesus' obedience, His conversation with the Father in the garden, His anguish. The reality of His pain is important. Grab your Bible again and flip to Hebrews 4:15 for an important reminder. What might have been Jesus' temptation in that garden? What is ours in our desperate pain? We have been given a perfect model here from a Savior who gets it. Our vulnerability is safe here, friend.

Chapter 10—Peace

1. Have you ever experienced peace that passes all understanding, peace that doesn't even make sense? Reflect on it and write it down. My dad suffered a heart attack this past summer that became a hard road of suffering for him, but the nurses' frequent comments to my parents those first harried days in the hospital were, "How are you so calm?" Palpable peace, peace that doesn't even make sense, can become a pretty loud testimony. In what ways would my parents have been able to answer? In what ways might you have responded?

2. Read John 14:25–27 in any translation. Then grab a different translation and read it again. Or look it up on a Bible website, such as Biblegateway.com. Who has Jesus left to teach us? How might He bring to remembrance these words?

3. This feels like a great spot to pray an invitation for more learning. If part of the Holy Spirit's job is to

teach and call to remembrance, let's ask for a front-row seat for that education. Let's ask Him to make us keenly aware of His presence that we might be better students of all He teaches. What else might you pray for as you consider peace and courage?

Chapter 11—Worship

1. How do you define worship? Go back and reread Wayne Grudem's definition of worship on page 104. Does God's character change when life gets bumpy, difficult, or unpredictable? Why is it sometimes harder to worship here?

2. Read Psalm 96 and think through the concept of worship. What limits have you put on worship without even realizing? Is it a few songs in the Sunday service? Is it a music genre? Test those limits in Scripture—what might worship really mean?

3. Look back at the four key takeaways we learned when studying Psalm 56:3—"When I am afraid, I will trust in You"—in context. Write them down. Tuck them on a note and slip it next to that verse in your Bible. Which one most connects with you? Why? Which one do you have the most difficulty embracing?

Chapter 12—Hope

1. Adaptability is not a bad thing—it's often helpful—but when our source of hope is rooted in our own ability to adjust, we build a faith that rests solely on . . . *us*. In what ways have you seen that? It becomes a weak anchor. Where might you have trusted your own ability

to pivot, to put on a happy face, rather than trusting God's greater plan and purpose, His ability to grow something good, even here?

2. Write these words down and then speak them aloud. *This is worth it. This is good, because God is growing something beautiful and rich here and I do not stand alone.* This is a brave and bold declaration of faith, friend. We can say this, believe this, because we know who He is and how He works. His Word confirms that He works all things for good (Romans 8:28), that even what may have been meant for evil He can use for good (Genesis 50:20). Choosing brave is choosing to take Him at His Word. In what ways do you need to choose brave, remember truth, and cling to hope today?

3. Romans 5:1–5 is a powerful passage, a powerful tool to have at your disposal, in your memory. Consider memorizing it now. Write it out and text a friend and ask her to memorize it with you. It's five verses. What do those verses mean for your life?

Chapter 13—Humility

1. Look up Hannah's story in 1 Samuel 1. Read it slowly and carefully. At what point in the story did Hannah's disposition change? Before or after what we acknowledge as the miracle?

2. "Whether our understanding of God is weak or robust, we put it all on trial something fast in tough times. How we are invested in Him now, today, matters more than we know." Let's test this, work this muscle. Set a timer for three minutes and write as many truths as you can about the character and nature of our heavenly

Father. As you keep studying, reading, and learning about God, keep adding to this list. Fill a page or a book. This is knowledge you need at the ready. This is who He is and you desperately need to remember it. Looking over your list, what do these character traits instill within you?

3. In 1 Peter we learned that God resists—some translations say *opposes*—the proud, but gives grace to the humble. Don't breeze past that stark contrast, friend. Scripture goes on to say that He exalts at the proper time. Oh, the ambiguity of that term, *proper time,* is a tough pill to swallow at times, isn't it? But there is no ambiguity with our God. He asks for cares, our concerns, and worries because He cares about us right here in our proper time of waiting. The waiting is always made easier by the proper position of our hearts. What proper time do you need to humbly lay before Him?

Chapter 14—Heritage

1. Brainstorm some practical ways you can "not lose sight of His greatness, His realness, in the midst of your normal." Distraction is real. Forgetfulness is real. But what practices and habits help you, as Corrie ten Boom says, keep big things big and small things small?

2. Where have you seen God's grace and provision in your own heritage and history? It may be in your family of origin. It may be through mentors or godly leaders He has placed in your life. It may be a pastor or a friend. Take a moment to be intentional about seeing His provision and thanking Him for it.

3. Psalm 145:4 says, "One generation shall praise Your works to another, and shall declare Your mighty acts." Are we active participants in this? What does your life praise and declare? What are you passing on to the next generation walking close at your heels? May it be Christ, friend. Above all else, may it be Christ.

Chapter 15—Community

1. Think back over your experiences with community both inside and outside the church. What have been some of the highs and lows? When or where have you seen it done well?

2. "The beauty of community is directly dependent on how you navigate the bumps and bruises it produces." We often balk at these bumps and bruises. We see them as the failure of community. And sometimes they are. But what if they can also provide growth and beauty that builds bonds and fosters Christlike responsiveness in all of us? What if bumps and bruises are actually opportunity? How do you reflexively respond to bumps and bruises in community?

3. "Don't fear the messiness of community, fear God." Have you ever had a negative experience with community? Why do you think this statement is true? No matter where you are on that journey, how life-giving or suffocating it has been, take a minute to acknowledge your struggles with engaging in community. Thank Him for His beautiful design and the gift of community. Ask Him to give you the courage to trust, to be vulnerable, to work through hard things. Ask Him to give you holy courage no matter what your history might be

because you know who He is, how He works, and that He can use it all.

Chapter 16—Give Me Grace

1. Think about John Newton's famous words from "Amazing Grace": "'Twas grace that taught my heart to fear and grace my fears relieved." Chances are, you know this song, you have sung it. You may even have it memorized. But what does that line mean?
2. Has grace become timely or trendy? And if so, at the expense of what?
3. How might we espouse a proper fear of the Lord not at the expense of grace, but at a fuller understanding of it?

Chapter 17—Necessity

1. Think of a time that took incredible mental focus or physical strength for you. A race you ran, physical pain you endured, a test you studied for. What would it look like to apply those faculties toward loving God, fully, completely—with all you have, choosing to adore Him?
2. How have you viewed mentions of the fear of the Lord prior to now? In what ways are your perception and understanding changing?
3. This is the fun part, seeing the Scripture for yourself. Scan through some of the verses noted in this chapter or go dig for yourself. You will likely be surprised what you find when you start noticing! Begin in Psalms or Proverbs, Old Testament or New. Just take notice, don't run past it and get to dusting! What do you find that

most sticks out to you as you consider courage coming from fearing the Lord?

Chapter 18—Intimacy

1. God is big and close. It can be hard to hold the expanse of both those concepts in our minds. Which do you find easier to wrap your mind around—His greatness or His nearness? Why?
2. What are your "fear-tainted questions" about intimacy with God? What holds you back?
3. Have you ever had a cymbal-ring moment of your own? Have you held back or hid instead of drawing near to the One who, yes, we fear and yet who loves us more than we can comprehend? This is safe, friend. This is intimacy.

Chapter 19—Freedom

1. What ill-fitting, weighed-down overalls have you worn? Which ones are you currently wearing?
2. "If truth is really true, then it must be true *for us. In us.* Backstory, hard past, or hard present notwithstanding." This sentence bears repeating. Have you disqualified yourself from truth at times? Believed it firmly for others, yet doubted His goodness in your own story?
3. Paul declared it—it is for freedom that Christ set us free (see Galatians 5:1). We are no longer slaves to a yoke of bondage. Christ paid the ultimate price for our freedom in order that we may do just that—live free. He is our strength and our courage, our fear and our freedom. How does this/should this change how you live out your days?

Acknowledgments

It feels more than a little disingenuous to have so many people lend themselves to your life, your work, and your words and then put your name alone on the cover. They all should be there, because in the midst of how these page have been both lived and written, they were there.

To my praying team: Deon, Lois, Deb, Sharon, Linda, Herminia, Doris, Melissa, and Nora. There is no greater gift than to have someone you know, someone who knows you, ready and willing to pray. You have been a safe and honest place for me. Your prayers have fitted me, carried me. Thank you for storming heaven on my behalf. You have helped carry this work in ways the world will never know, but I do. And He does. Thank you.

My life group, church, and extended family—your interest and excitement, and, even more, your prayers, have fitted and strengthened me for the task. Thank you.

To Don, who believed in this book before I did. Thank you for your wisdom and insight. Thank you for guiding me wisely and leading me well. And to Tawny, for joining me, stepping in mid-stream. Unknown territory always feels scary, but you both have been good and safe guides—His gift to a girl who's new here.

To Jennifer, you might be the closest I'll ever come to winning a jackpot. Your enthusiasm is my favorite. To Ginger, you have been an indispensable teacher. Thank you to the entire Bethany team for taking me under your wing and shepherding this book with integrity.

To the friends God has given me on this journey, especially when I didn't know a single soul who did this kind of work. Krista and Alex and the whole Sisterhood, Lisa and the Club 31 Women, you have mentored and trained and cheered me on. Learning from and with you is God's great kindness to me.

Debbi Perkins, thank you for being my first mentor, for drawing me out, and pushing me to tell my story. Lisa, thank you for being a continual mentor and one of the safest places to ask questions. I'm so thankful for you. Herminia, you have been a true and constant example of loving and living for Christ. Deon, there aren't even words for the unexpected gift of your friendship, but I know it's a unique and precious gift. You continue to bless me.

Kelli and Sara—more unexpected gifts. You point me to the Father through the realness of our lives and callings.

To my friends on the ground, nearby—the ones who know how often I burn the bread I'm toasting for dinner, have seen me cry real tears, and have lived through all the stories I may never write about. You have grown me more than you even realize. You are gifted and called in ways far different from me and yet God knew I would need you desperately—to lean on and learn from and grow with. Your presence in my life is a gift that could only come from Him. Only He orchestrates such beautiful things. Jo, Chelsea, Michelle, Beth, Marta, Janess, Bree and so many more who have texted Scripture and encouragement. You are all life-giving.

Candee and Alesha, you have seen it all. Know it all. And love so well. You make me braver. Thank you for praying me through.

Dan and Candee. Friends who are family. You have supported, celebrated, and grown these words. Your ministry to our family, in ways both big and small, has been nothing short of His grace, extravagant. We love you.

How do you thank parents who have invested their lives and never stopped? Mom and Dad, thank you for believing, for never doubting, for cheering. Thank you for owning every ounce of your role and sacrificing to make this work possible. But mostly, thank you for introducing me to Jesus and showing me what it's like to follow Him.

To Tyler, Baily, Brooklyn, and Bo—my heritage. Thank you for sharing your mama with joy (most of the time), for being wise beyond your years, and being the greatest tool by which God continues to grow me and make me braver. You are a gift.

Ali Jo, I can't wait to meet you, fighter girl. I'm grateful for your life.

To Ross. Of all the unexpected gifts, you are the greatest. Thank you for making space for this project, for believing in this, and for "fixing it" when I get weary. You are a loyal defender and protector. And I understand God's love, care, and mercy even more because of the way you live it out beside me.

And to God. You blow my mind and I know I've only skimmed the surface. Your provision has astounded me. Thank you for the many ways you keep teaching me. Give me the courage to keep drawing nearer still. Be my all. My hands are wide open. It's all for you.

Chapter 1: The Truth about Fear

1. Lewis Carroll, *Alice's Adventures in Wonderland* (New York: Charles E. Merrill Company, 1911), 9.

2. "Fear," Merriam Webster, https://www.merriam-webster.com/diction ary/fear.

Chapter 2: What Do I Know of Holy?

1. Mayberry is the idyllic, fictional small town from *The Andy Griffith Show* of the 1960s.

2. Isaiah 6:3.

3. Isaiah 6:8.

Chapter 4: Good-Bye Fearlessness

1. NLT.

2. Hebrews 5:7, emphasis added.

3. Hebrews 5, Bible Study Tools, accessed December 17, 2019, https://www.biblestudytools.com/commentaries/matthew-henry-complete/heb rews/5.html/.

Chapter 5: Someone Worth Fearing

1. Paul David Tripp, *Awe: Why It Matters For Everything We Think, Say and Do* (Wheaton, IL: Crossway, 2015), 30.

Chapter 6: Smaller Gods

1. See Genesis 22.
2. See Genesis 16.
3. See Exodus 2.
4. See 1 Samuel 1.
5. See Luke 1.
6. Jen Wilkin, *None Like Him: Ten Ways God Is Different From Us* (Wheaton, IL: Crossway), 48.
7. Ephesians 2:9.
8. Marshall Segal, "How Not to Be Desperate," *Desiring God*, February 27, 2019, https://www.desiringgod.org/articles/how-not-to-be-desperate.
9. Carl Boberg, "How Great Thou Art," copyright ©1885.

Chapter 7: On Trend

1. A.W. Tozer, *The Knowledge of the Holy: The Attributes of God, Their Meaning in the Christian Life* (New York: Harper & Row, 1961), 9.

Chapter 9: Vulnerability

1. "Vulnerable," Merriam Webster, https://www.merriam-webster.com/dictionary/vulnerable.
2. 1 Samuel 13:14.
3. Matthew 26:38.
4. Luke 22:44.
5. Elisabeth Elliot, *Suffering Is Never for Nothing* (Nashville: B&H Publishing, 2019), 15.

Chapter 10: Peace

1. Pam Rosewell Moore, *The Five Silent Years of Corrie ten Boom* (Grand Rapids: Zondervan, 1986), 139.

Chapter 11: Worship

1. Wayne Grudem, *Systematic Theology* (Grand Rapids, MI: Zondervan, 1994), 1011.
2. NLT.
3. NLT.
4. Luke 7:36–50.

Chapter 12: Hope

1. *Vine's Complete Expository Dictionary* (Nashville, TN: Thomas Nelson, 1996), 311. Not a direct quote.

Chapter 13: Humility

1. Matthew Henry, "An Exposition, with Practical Observations, of the First Book of Samuel, Chapter 1," *Blue Letter Bible*, accessed December 17, 2019, https://www.blueletterbible.org/Comm/mhc/1Sa/1Sa_001.cfm?a =237010.
2. Genesis 3:5.

Chapter 16: Give Me Grace

1. *Vine's Complete Expository*, 277.
2. Proverbs 13:12.
3. A.W. Tozer, *The Terror of the Lord,* accessed December 17, 2019, http://www.acts17-11.com/snip_tozer_terror.html.
4. Tozer, *The Terror of the Lord.*
5. 1 Peter 1:13 ESV.
6. 1 Peter 1:16 ESV.

Chapter 17: Necessity

1. Emphasis added.
2. Job 28:28 CSB.

Chapter 18: Intimacy

1. Paul David Tripp, *Come, Let Us Adore Him* (Wheaton, IL: Crossway, 2017), 44.

Chapter 19: Freedom

1. Matthew 9.
2. Luke 7:36–50.
3. C.S. Lewis, *The Lion, the Witch and the Wardrobe* (New York: Harper Collins, 1978), 81.
4. Galatians 5:16.
5. Galatians 5:18.
6. Galatians 5:25.
7. Matthew 6:8.

Afterword

1. Revelation 15:3–4 CSB, Revelation 22:20.

About the Author

Katie Westenberg blogs at I Choose Brave (www.ichoosebrave. com) and contributes regularly to Club 31 Women, iBelieve, Kirk Cameron's The Courage, and Motherly. She has been published with *The Huffington Post*, *The Unveiled Wife*, and Beating 50 Percent. Katie is passionate about speaking truth and encouraging women to use their gifts bravely for the glory of their Creator. Katie was born, raised, and still resides in Washington State. She and her husband are raising four kids ages six to thirteen.